BBC MUSIC GUIDES

BRAHMS SONGS

BBC MUSIC GUIDES

Brahms Songs

ERIC SAMS

UNIVERSITY OF WASHINGTON PRESS
SEATTLE

Contents

First published 1972 by the British Broadcasting Corporation
Copyright © Eric Sams 1972
University of Washington Press edition first published 1972
Library of Congress Catalog Card Number 72-552
ISBN 0-295-95250-4
Printed in England

Introduction

The *Lied* as an art-form arises when words inspire music which embodies them, just as a face or scene might move another artist to paint a portrait or landscape. So it is not necessarily the greatest poems that make the best *Lieder,* any more than it is the most beautiful faces or landscapes that make the best pictures. What matters is the quality of feeling distilled into the finished work of art. This comparison is especially apt to Brahms, whose song-themes are love and nature and whose penchant is for second-rate verses on those themes. There are two reasons for that predilection. First, his passion for reading was self-determined, and his appreciation of it self-taught; and he could never tell good verse from bad, or folk from fake. Secondly, and more important, he was above all a musician, seeking an outlet through poetry for his own feeling. His songs are always ready to turn into instrumental music; it is no mere chance that so many of them are echoed in his violin sonatas, nor that they contain so much long-flighted melody and contrapuntal device.

Thus Brahms inhabits that hinterland of the *Lied* where song borders on absolute music, while Hugo Wolf occupies the opposite frontier where song aspires to the condition of poetry or recitation. No wonder there was no love lost between them. No wonder either that they had no clear or immediate successors as great song-writers; each had explored his own domain to its farthest limits. Each had inherited his portion from Schumann, who as successor to Schubert had become the undisputed sovereign of that realm where words and music meet and mingle in lyric forms. That territory was a microcosm of the social world of Europe. It had derived from a new movement in German poetry. With Goethe and Hölty, verse had become singable, as if classical style and metre had been crossed with folksong. At the same time the pianoforte was being developed as an accompanying instrument, again a compromise between the court orchestra and the homely guitar. Thus the romantic nineteenth-century *Lied* began with Schubert as a middle-class hybrid form, blending elevated style with popular feeling.

Brahms was Schubert's heir. He had little of the musico-poetic depth and complexity of Wolf or Schumann. Conversely, they wrote no popular music of their own, while he was so steeped in that tradition that his songs became not only popular music but 'folksong' in his own lifetime, like 'Wiegenlied' or 'Vergebliches Ständchen'. So (by then) had many of Schubert's, and their *Lieder* are strikingly akin, especially in their use of melody, which was for them the heart of song-writing. Both favoured strophic forms where successive verses are repeated to the same tune. So general a treatment is bound to be less apt for some stanzas than for others and will lead to occasional incongruities such as the faulty declamation for which both have been criticised. The price seems little enough for a great song. Even if Brahms goes further than others there are always compensations. Here for example are the rhythmically simple first two lines of a Hölty quatrain:

> Holder klingt der Vogelsang,
> Wenn die Engelreine . . .

(literally, and metrically, Sweéter soúnds the sóng of bírds
> Whén the ángel-púre one . . .)

as set by (*a*) Schubert (1816), (*b*) Mendelssohn (*c*. 1826), (*c*) Brahms (completed 1877):

Ex. 1

Mendelssohn could hardly have known the Schubert setting, which was not published until 1885. Each represents a basic and obvious melodic equivalent of the verses. Brahms probably knew the Mendelssohn setting, if not the Schubert. But he preferred a more complex type of melody; his wayward and cross-grained treatment of Hölty's text is not the least successful or engaging of these three delightful songs.

In matters of construction, however, Brahms was a thoroughgoing Schubertian. Nearly half his songs are strophic, whether *simpliciter* or with variations. Most of the rest are basically in A B A form. They evince no special interest in the poetic or literary aspects of song. The rich vocabulary of accompaniment figurations and rhythms is deployed to give formal variety, just as in the instrumental music, rather than as conscious illustration of the verse. We rarely hear the words for their own sake, as recitative; they are more a medium for melody. Even so, the vocal line is often restrained in its compass and intervals. Only two songs ('Klage I', 'Frühlingslied') call for a rising major seventh; only one (the last of all) requires a vocal leap of more than a tenth, and then only as an alternative. Similarly the traditional harmony is not enriched, as Wolf's was, with Wagnerian coinages; their small change, such as the augmented triad, was hardly ever tendered by Brahms. There is little rhythmical experimentation apart from the frequent use of two-against-three, and this too is usually more an instrumental device than expression of verbal ideas. Entirely typical is Brahms's advice to an aspiring song-writer to 'make sure that together with your melody you compose a strong independent bass'. Indeed, his method of judging songs was to cover up everything but these two lines, as if song were essentially a construction of melody and counterpoint. Certainly these are the most easily identifiable of his own fingerprints. For example, the piano's horn passages in the early songs, though striking and characteristic, are not so clearly and unmistakably Brahmsian as the voice's rising or falling dominant seventh arpeggios in the middle period songs:

Ex. 2

(a) *An die Nachtigall*   (b) *An ein Veilchen II*

lieb - ent - flammten Lie- der   dei -nem blau- en Kel - che.

or the ubiquitous falling sixths or sevenths at the final cadence of songs about the bliss and sweetness of love:

Ex. 3

(a) (c. 1864)   (b) (1877)

Sü — sse   sel — ber ist   wei — ssen Hals   mir

(c) (1885)   (d) (1896)

i   hab   di   so   lieb   (Die Liebe ist die grösseste)   un — ter   ih —   nen

Hugo Wolf would no doubt have disputed the Brahmsian view, claiming that songs were not so much musical as musico-poetic; that declamation, rhythm, keyboard register and texture, and motivic treatment were fully as important as melody; and that they all ought to derive from the poem. Fortunately that dispute is over, and we can learn from both masters and both schools. Most song-writers will agree that music symbolises human feeling. For Brahms, the absolute musician, the succession and structure of tones does this without any special or conscious need for adaptation. Clearly this attitude was due to innate temperament, not to any lack of technique or inspiration. Further, his earliest published works were pseudonymous pianoforte pot-pourris of operatic airs and national songs, so he had plenty of practice in writing accompanied melody. Even in his early piano sonatas the slow-movement melodies often derive from the metrical movement of a poem or song that had caught his fancy. No doubt many of Brahms's other works throughout his life contain melodies suggested to him by his reading of verse.

Although *Lieder* form a natural part of his development from eighteen onwards his settings are a response to a general mood rather than to poetry as such. This is clear from his repetitions of the text for the sole purpose of sustaining the melodic line. Such a viewpoint, though dismaying to the purist, has its own practical advantages and its own real insights. For example, it was always possible for Brahms to find a poem which suited his mood and then to clothe it with ready-made material. This was often an arduous and time-consuming process; but it could also be a very successful one.

In any event, the choice of verse will tell us much of interest about Brahms as man and musician. He had at his disposal a wide range of German poetry, which by the nineteenth century included some of the outstanding masterpieces of world literature. If from this whole rich field he culled mainly such nonentities as Lemcke or Daumer, it was for excellent personal reasons. That pulp was the right raw material for his creative process, which was powered by his own inmost feelings. So when he sings for example of two lovers parting (as in Opp. 14 and 19 *passim*) or of their walking together in the woodlands ('Wir wandelten', 'In Waldeseinsamkeit') he is likely to be recalling some experienced emotion, probably on some actual occasion, and using some later more tranquil time to

8

turn that emotion into music. Thus he chooses texts as a preacher might – less for their intrinsic merit than for relevance to a given topic or mood. Other composers set the words; Brahms uses them to set the tone, or the scene, of his own experience. But to describe his songs thus is not to disparage them. They contain deep and valid symbols of felt life, true experience, as real and durable as any ever expressed by a composer.

The animating force, in Brahms as in all the great song-writers, is the musical image. The following examples seek to illustrate only the two extremes of a very wide spectrum from the presumably unconscious to the clearly deliberate. An example of the former is the idea of vision or dream expressed in slow upward arpeggios in the left hand, like a vague notion drifting up from sleep towards the borderlands of consciousness, as throughout 'Es träumte mir':

Ex. 4

and similarly throughout 'Es hing ein Reif', which has the direction 'träumerisch', or to illustrate the word 'Traum' in 'Der Tod, das ist die kühle Nacht'. This idea begins with that fine song 'An eine Aeolsharfe' where the Aeolian harp symbolises the sensitive mind caught in a trance through which the least breath turns into music.

A conscious form of translation is the equally Schumannian technique of turning names into expressive musical symbols letter by letter. Brahms is known to have used that device in the String Sextet, Op. 36, and the a cappella chorus, Op. 44, no. 10, where the name Agathe (von Siebold) becomes:

Ex. 5

A G A H E

I shall suggest that he also used this idea in the solo songs written for Agathe, and further that an analogous idea can help to identify those songs which were written with Clara Schumann especially in mind.

Between these two realms of subconscious and conscious invention, whole regions lie open to research and conjecture. Perhaps the best way of examining this musical vocabulary in detail is to consider a song chosen as typical by Brahms himself, in his early forties, when advising an aspiring song-writer. He is recorded as saying that one must not be too easily satisfied. The first ideas or inspirations, whatever or whenever one calls them, come of their own accord or not at all. When they do, then the real work begins. They are not really our property until we have worked on them, cultivated them, made them our own. This will not be quick or easy. Take for example the beginning of 'Die Mainacht' (here Brahms sang the first line). Having got that far, he said, 'I might as well shut the book, go for a walk, do absolutely anything; even forget the whole thing for six months. But if it is a live and viable idea, then in the meantime it will be growing unseen. Then I can begin work on it.'

One may venture to reconstruct the process. Brahms says in effect that he had a book of Hölty's poems open in front of him. 'Die Mainacht' is in four stanzas of a classical metre (asclepiads), the first of which may be rendered thus to show meaning and metre together:

Now the silvery moon gleams among boughs and leaves,
Strewing slumberous light over the dreaming lawn.
Sweet the nightingale's fluting;
Sad my walking from tree to tree.

The next two stanzas compare and contrast shared nest and sweet song with lonely silence, darker shadows. Finally the poem declares the cause of its sorrow: 'I shall never see you on earth again, my love; and the scalding tears flow faster yet'. Hölty's opening lines repeat the same thought and the same metrical pattern; so the natural response would be to repeat the melody with some variation, say a tone higher. Then comes a modulation with flats to match the flutes, and finally a sad minor melodic line to match the last poetic line. In this way the natural growth of the music will conform with the lattice work of the poem's pattern of meaning and metre. But other influences are also soon at work. For example the stately $3 + 3, 3 + 3$ beat of the classic foot has to move in duple or quadruple time, because of the poetic image of walking and its musical equivalent. This is incorporated into the piano part, which duly begins with the vocal melody set walking in a separate prelude. When the nightingales' fluting mellows the melody into a different key, the piano's left-hand accents, gentle though they are, have to be elided:

Ex. 6

und   die   Nach - ti - gall   flö — — tet

only to reappear as the walking resumes in a sombre E flat minor, this time serving as an illustrative piano interlude. Next, the piano left hand has detached thirds for the dewy foliage (a typical Brahmsian expression) while the right hand makes a cooing duo with the voice for the billing doves. The left-hand arpeggios of trance or dream (cf. Ex. 4) anticipate the longed-for vision of the last verse, and therefore sound dramatic and tragic. Canonic imitations signify a parting of the ways at the voice's recitative 'I turn away', while at the following phrase 'and seek darker shadows' the music reverts to the darkness of E flat minor, always a sombre key in Brahms as in Schumann. There the hollow unison of voice and piano re-echoes and stresses the feeling of personal isolation, again a very Brahmsian expression. It moves to tears; and for the first time the quavers flow uninterruptedly in the right hand, with a sharp semitonal clash on the word 'Tränen'. There follows a dramatic pause as the piano dwells lingeringly on the dominant seventh; and this focuses the emotive radiance of the music thus far on to the burning question – why? The answer coincides with the return of the opening melody, and the singing vision of un-returned and unreturning love. This time (again very typically) the accompaniment is given added rhythmic interest; the pulse of the music and of the singer quicken together. Again the tears flow, with the same poignant dissonance as before, this time even more readily and explicably in conformity with the sense of the words. The crying climax comes on a chord of the flat supertonic which always conveys a special sense of tragedy and loss in a Brahms song. The piano postlude continues its walking movement, in which the depressed mood of tears and sighs is matched by flattened sevenths, flattened sixths; the music goes weeping away into the dark.

If one likes romantic verse heightened and intensified by music, here is its perfect expression. But despite all its subconscious yearning and intuitive art this music contains much conscious device. All the formal effects had to be closely and deliberately calculated. For example Brahms aims at a basic ABA form; so one stanza out of four has to be omitted. He reasons that his music need say only once that (to borrow the equivalent phrases of an English late-Romantic, Francis Thompson):

> I walk, I only,
> Not I only wake;
> Nothing is, this sweet night,
> But doth couch and wake
> For its love's sake.

This leaves three stanzas with three different ideas: (1) loneliness, (2) togetherness, (3) lost love. The last of these ideas, in contrasting with the second, explains the first. So the musical material equates (1) with (3) and contrasts each with (2); the perfect ABA form.

In other ways too the constructional problems are solved with superb eloquence. The first verse began by saying 'bright moonlight'; the second ended by saying 'and I weep'. The music of that first phrase is repeated at the words 'when shall I see her smile again'; of the second at the words 'and the tears flow faster yet'. This gives each repetition a double force, contrasting bright presence with bright absence and adding tears to tears. Again, the whole song is given logical and constructional unity by the left-hand minims and right-hand quavers, moving in solemn progression through the quiet night. Yet this idea is heard in only sixteen bars out of fifty-one. Elsewhere the accompaniment rhythm, figuration and texture are constantly varied and refined, stressing and underlining the words without ever distracting attention from the forward movement of the song as a whole.

Such variation is a Brahmsian fingerprint. It is often hard to detect because the surface texture of the music has been so carefully joined and polished. Thus in the dovetailing here from lone bush to shared nest the quaver accompaniment passes from right hand to left in the smoothest of transitions. Soon afterwards comes a return to the shadows; and again a minimal change of texture and register (left-hand arpeggios) alters the whole complexion of the accompaniment. Then, as the song flows imperturbably on, the repeated chords in which the doves duet in the dew are gradually reabsorbed into the texture of the music, as that memory fades again into the surrounding darkness. This ceaselessly changing variety packs the music full of ideas, making it sound through-composed, bar by bar. The basic simplicity of melody, harmony and form is worked and developed into living complexity. We can hear the organic process, in one sense, just as Brahms described it – like the germination of seed-corn, to use his own simile. But the ground also had to be tilled and nourished with unremitting toil; and this too is often audible. The good grain sustains and delights all Brahms-lovers; the palpable effort inherent in its cultivation is what his detractors hear and hate. He became and remained a master by being the servant, indeed the slave, of his art; and his songs are 'works' in the most meaningful sense. They present a fine likeness of the man; and they contain some of the world's finest masterpieces in the genre.

One would expect from a composer of Brahms's stature that all his themes and their developments, verbal and musical, should grow and mature with the years. The contrary view is perhaps more widely held. Frank Walker and Walter Legge go so far as to say (in their perceptive notes to the famous Kipnis record album made for the Brahms Song Society formed in 1936) that 'unlike Schubert and Wolf, Brahms as a song-writer did not develop materially in style as he grew older. . . . The style is essentially the same in the songs of Op. 3 or 7 as it is in the closing years of his life; there is virtually no discernible difference in manner of mental approach or technical handling between the products of the Brahms of twenty and the Brahms of sixty.' This, if true, marks him firmly down as a minor master of the *Lied*, on a par with Franz and Jensen. Certainly the case is a strong one, not easily rebutted. Brahms's songs do give exactly that impression. But the argument may sit more comfortably the other way round. Thus – he was a great song-writer; therefore his art developed; therefore if any of his late songs sound like early ones, a plausible explanation is that they in fact *are* early ones. This would require as a corollary some evidence that the songs were often drafted and then retained for polishing and further reflection, often for very long periods. Exactly this, on overwhelming evidence, was typical of Brahms in his songs as in all his work. Nothing short of perfection would do, whether it took twenty minutes or twenty years; or even if it had to be finally destroyed, as many a song was. His song-writing, even more than his normal compositional processes, was exacting and time-consuming, and he usually had some larger-scale work on hand, which demanded priority. For all these reasons, Brahms at sixty was certainly publishing work written mainly in his forties or even in his twenties; and in these circumstances he could hardly fail to create the impression of lack of development.

One sees what is meant by that criticism. The music flows always in the same channels. But these are worn not merely smoother but wider and deeper over the years, as can perhaps be shown by a series of chartings and soundings. The next two chapters seek to trace Brahms's song-writing back to its technical and emotional sources in his musical influences and personal affections, and to follow its course up to the emergence of his mainstream song-style. Thereafter the interest lies more in the changing landscape and climate of chosen poem and matching music; so the works of each successive song-writing phase are considered in the following order. First come the artefacts, i.e. songs constructed from, or containing, music already written; it is in these that Brahms the craftsman is best observed. Then come the love-songs grave or gay; these are the heart of the music, and they tell us much about Brahms the man. The serious love-songs seem to be mainly linked with Clara Schumann in their musical or poetic themes; and their prevailing mood is one of tender reverence. But even they pass through a phase of sensuality; and there is always a continuing strain of ironical or worldly songs. Gravity and gaiety alike lead through frustration and despair to the same sad final outcome, in disillusion or dissolution. Hence there is a third category of songs where words and music alike sing of escape and release, whether into the realms of nature, nostalgia, or death.

Of course the prevailing emotional climate changes with the year and the season. Naturally too the proposed classifications are not exclusive; the music is often at its most intense when two or more of these ideas coincide. Similarly they vary in their modes of presentation, from the salon song to the folksong. But these categories if not exclusive are exhaustive. Each original song Brahms wrote for solo voice and piano will occur at least once in such an analysis. Thus presented, they seem to tell in both words and music a clear story of youth, manhood, maturity and age, illustrative of progressively keener insights, deeper feelings, finer craftsmanship.

1852-58: Early Songs

Potential mastery is evident from the first. The earliest known song – 'Heimkehr', to words by Uhland (1851)[1] – sounds like the work of a young pianist who has found an appealing poem; its themes of love and a return home in fact dominate Brahms's song-writing all his life. His models are popular song-writers, and above all Schubert. Further, the hackwork of making piano pot-pourris has already provided the concept of grand opera, as confirmed by the hectic climax and repetitions, and a final triumphant chord inviting applause. Uhland's unpretentious and even ironical poem is being coerced into solemnity and grandeur, and so fails to respond as it should. Brahms in this melodramatic vein needed matching verse.

He was also ready for more song-experiments. The most direct was the piano piece with words, which Schumann had shown both by precept and example to be how pianists wrote songs. Melodrama and keyboard music combine in 'Lied aus Iwan', Op. 3, no. 4 (1853); but the hectic words are too obviously a mere veneer on the music, and maladroitly stuck on. A more fruitful in-fluence was Robert Franz, notable for his setting of folksong, a topic in which Brahms had always taken the keenest interest. 'Volkslied' and 'Die Trauernde' (both 1852) are in that style; the latter text was also set by Franz. Equally congenial was the influence of Mendelssohn. Brahms's 'Parole' (1853), a Schubertian song of sadness in springtime, begins with the same upward flourish as Mendelssohn's spring song 'Gruss'; 'Juchhe' (1852), also a spring song, echoes the latter's 'Frühlingslied', Op. 8; 'Nachwirkung' (1852) is thoroughly Mendelssohnian in mood and manner. But Brahms adds his own wilfulness and complexity – his 'Der Frühling' (1852) suffuses the sweet spring-song style with a headily aromatic waft of Wagner (reminding us that among the opera selections concocted by the young Brahms was one from *Tann-häuser*). The Hoffmann von Fallersleben poems of 'Liebe und Frühling I & II' (1853) have a more personal message for the

---

[1] For the given purpose the songs are discussed in order of composition, so far as possible. But Brahms rarely dated them, and often withheld them for revision over long periods; so there are bound to be areas of conjecture or approximation. The dates given are those of completion, if known: but the words 'or earlier' could usually be added.

composer; and so therefore has he for his listeners. Characteristically, the message is a cryptic one, to which Max Kalbeck, Brahms's good friend and best biographer, was later given the key.

The first song compares the thoughts of love twining around memories with the clinging tendrils of vine and convolvulus; and the music, too, gently entwists in canonic imitation. The young Brahms had been charmed by a girl who sang Zerlina in *Don Giovanni*. Perhaps he saw himself as Masetto, the blunt and sturdy peasant who lacks finesse with women. However this may be, we are assured that both songs contain a deliberate allusion to Zerlina's aria *Batti, batti*. Kalbeck does not illustrate this idea; but presumably this is meant:

Ex. 7
(a)   Andante   (transposed for comparison)

Bat – ti,   bat – ti o bel   Ma – set – to

(b)   Moderato

Mei – ne   Tag – und Nacht-ge – dank – en

As the melody imagines 'Zerlina', and sings of thoughts by night and day, the bass completes the simile by twining the themes of vine and convolvulus into the music. Nothing could be more Schumannian, yet this song was completed before the two had met. Those great minds thought alike because of an innate affinity.

The second 'Liebe und Frühling' song also presages the mature composer in its musical equivalents of nature-study. The idea of breezes and waves induces new movement in the piano part, which in the reprise is made tremulous with excitement by added rhythmical interest; and this formal device also is typical of the later Brahms. In general his style is set in these early songs, where the melodies are the main means of expression, as in the Eichendorff 'Lied' (c. 1853) which omits a whole rhyming line, presumably by mere inadvertence; Brahms from the first is setting verse for his own sake, not the poem's. This is also clear from the choice of text. Just as in Mendelssohn or Franz (or the later Schumann) masters like Uhland and Eichendorff are ranked with journeymen like Rousseau and Meissner; and all are treated with scant respect. But whenever good verse and receptive mood coincide, the result is delectable; as in the opening of 'Nachtigallen schwingen' (1853), again to words by Hoffmann, which begins with a memorable singing and soaring of quick yet long-flighted melody. In all this early work the inspiration is audibly drawn from folksong accompaniments as well as classical models. The ubiquitous horn passages (or sometimes parallel sixths, as in 'Wie die Wolke nach der Sonne', 1853) are clearly associated with the hunter or the chase, as in the middle section of 'Parole', where the grazing deer and the ominous shot in the dark remind the singer of her absent lover, himself a huntsman. By extension they evoke the open air or the countryside in general. Hence perhaps their relevance in the Eichendorff song 'Anklänge' (1853), which begins 'High over the silent hills stands a house in the woods'. Predictably, the same symbol occurs in 'Spanisches Lied' (1852), as the girl's hair is blown about in the wind. But this stock response hardly detracts from an otherwise inspired song with melodic ideas so engaging in themselves and so interlocked with the lyric as to rival Wolf's setting ('In dem Schatten meiner Locken'). The perplexed yet happy thoughts of love are turned into a sedate fandango with puzzled harmonies gently soothed, just as in Wolf, and with an added sense of counterpoint and structure. The whole material, melody and accompaniment alike, is an elaboration of the same basic pattern, woven from subtle threads of hinted unhappiness and frustration. In particular the falling arpeggios recall other sadder songs of separation; 'Treue Liebe' (c. 1853), 'Parole' (c. 1853) and later 'Muss es eine Trennung geben' (1868) from the *Magelone-Lieder*.

All the most fruitful influences and ideas of these themes – lost love, undying fidelity, Schubertian melody, Brahmsian counterpoint, quasi-operatic solo and duet, keyboard solo and accompaniment, expressive rhythms and tonality – ripen together in the masterpiece of the early songs, 'Liebestreu' (1853). This is essentially a reworking, by a more mature and accomplished composer, of the first known song, 'Heimkehr'. It has the same repeated chords, the same canonic devices, the same dramatic climax. The poet's dialogue between mother and daughter not only permits strong musical contrasts but also (as is evident from later songs) made a strong personal appeal to Brahms. For sheer musical gift and intellectual force in a young composer nothing had been heard like it since Schubert – whose 'Erlkönig' and 'Gretchen' had been inspired by magnificent poetry, whereas Brahms's triumph is achieved despite Reinick's sentimental magazine rhymes. The poet's main contribution was a title which happened to strike the vital keynote of Brahms's song-writing; and perhaps of his whole being. But Reinick also offers a metaphor of the weight and depth of grief which is suitable for translation into musical terms.

The whole song matches the poetic image of a shed sorrow first falling like a stone into the depths of the sea, and then rising uncontrollably despite its weight because it insists on returning to the surface of consciousness, refusing to be forgotten. All these contrasts, and more, are compressed into ten bars of highly unified music. Perhaps the music is over-rhetorical for its text, even melodramatic; and this, together with its reliance on the memories of 'Heimkehr', arguably detracts from its total achievement. But the young Brahms was right to choose it to stand at the forefront of his published songs, in fulfilment of his earnest wish to be worthy of Robert Schumann's confidence and admiration. The choice may also have reflected this song's part in bringing about their fateful encounter. Of all the works Brahms had brought to Joachim in 1853 this had made the profoundest impression. It showed that here was a master musician potentially as great as Schumann, to whom Brahms was accordingly dispatched with the warmest possible recommendation.

What followed is well-known history. First came a few months of blissful happiness with his new-found friends Robert and Clara, both kindred spirits. Schumann hailed the young Johannes in print, in the most extravagant and fulsome terms, as 'he that should come'. This testimony, supplemented by introductions to publishers, laid enduring foundations of public success and acclaim and also of private jealousy and resentment from other musicians. Then in February 1854 tragedy struck. Schumann's disease reached his brain and left him a helpless mental cripple at forty-three, doomed to deteriorate to death within two years. The burden of caring and providing for the family fell on the thirty-four-year-old Clara, desperate with grief and pregnant with their eighth child. Brahms at twenty saw it as his plain duty to stay in Düsseldorf and give what help he could. He had been admired and befriended by two of the foremost musicians in the world, a great composer and a great pianist; so as man and musician he was bound to the Schumanns, man and wife, not only by affection and gratitude but by the whole tradition of his art. And of course he fell in love with

Clara, who in turn loved him deeply and was also devoted to her husband until the day of his death and to his memory thereafter. The vortex of this emotional maelstrom became the centre of Brahms's creative life. As his thoughts turned round the Schumann home and family, so did his music.

On the latter evidence, his love for Clara sought only spiritual expression at this stage. Otherwise he would surely have written love-songs for her as he later did for Agathe Siebold. They were his natural utterance; and he was as unselfconsciously outspoken in his music as in his choice of texts. But at first his feelings were those of adoration expressible not so much in love-songs as in hymns or songs of praise; and these belong more naturally to choral or instrumental forms. Hence, for example, the first version of the Piano Trio, Op. 8, with what seem to be its B minor and major Clara-themes and its quotations from Beethoven's *An die ferne Geliebte* cycle, all in the style of Schumann, together with other quotations, e.g. from Schubert ('Am Meer'), also suggesting that Clara and her loves and sorrows were enshrouding Brahms's whole life.[1] Similarly the C minor Piano Quartet, Op. 60, was written in the same thraldom, as he himself later confided. The other anguish, at the tragic fate of his hero Schumann, found an outlet in the music of the D minor Piano Concerto, and some of the darker themes of the Requiem. The whole tumultuous mood and story of those Düsseldorf days, sympathy, despair, love and final resolution and strength, seem to go into the First Symphony. But all these works took many years to reach their final form. It was as if the music had been stunned and driven inward by the shock of the Schumann tragedy. Song, as the most clearly personally expressive of all genres, suffered most grievously. The inspiration which had culminated so promisingly in 'Liebestreu' now became stultified and stifled by obsession with the Schumanns.

For example, the two Eichendorff songs 'In der Fremde' (1852) and 'Mondnacht' (1854) are settings of words taken not from the poet's text but from Schumann's settings of them, and in all good faith embody his textual alterations. Further, they are exactly in Schumann's style; the piano calls the tune which the voice in effect accompanies. So slavish a dependence for both words and music was inhibiting even though it was meant as homage.

Later, Clara's plight may have begun to dominate Brahms's

[1] 'Brahms and his Clara themes', *Musical Times,* May 1971.

musical mind. The spirited ballad 'Das Lied vom Herrn von Falkenstein', Op. 43, no. 4, is usually dated 1857. But all nine verses of it are about a woman's devotion to a loved one locked away in a cell by stern decree. True, the cell is an ordinary dungeon, the captor a mere tyrant. But the constant burden of the woman's voice pleading 'release my prisoner . . . I shall surely go out of my mind unless I see him again' was also the burden of Clara's letters to Brahms and others for two years, and the song may well have provided, consciously or not, a sympathetic echo for that voice. Much magnificent music lies locked inside it; a fine finale theme for a symphony came to a sad end here. Similarly 'Liebesklage des Mädchens', published in 1868 as Op. 48, no. 3, is also a song about a weeping woman, another image that must have been indelibly stamped in Brahms's sensitive mind. 'Who would see two living springs should behold my sad eyes,' she sings, 'who would behold deep wounds should see my wounded heart.' It begins with a theme which seems to have signified 'Clara' to Schumann; and it is written in a style so like his as to border on parody; almost every note in the voice is immediately echoed in the piano. Both those songs were, I suggest, written c. 1855.

So was 'Der Überläufer', Op. 48, no. 2, on similar musical and poetic themes, and also in the piano-song style of Schumann. There are two other early songs, where the musical interest and invention seem so slight and so derivative as to suggest that the words as such had some personal significance for Brahms. If so, he is heard changing his tune; for in both the theme turns from despair at losing an adored soul-mate to grief at losing a new-found love. In 'Vom verwundeten Knaben' a girl walking in the woods finds a badly wounded boy who soon dies despite her tender care. In 'Murrays Ermordung' again a young man dies, this time mourned by a queen. Those songs seem to presage a second bereavement for Clara. Brahms had to find his own way, make his own life, write his own music; and perhaps his choice of texts embodies this feeling. If so, both would have been written c. 1856. Their folksong texts, like those of the other two mentioned above, were to be found in Schumann's library; many of his books came to Brahms, either on loan or as gifts from Clara.

In later years, in a more propitious emotional climate, that seed would flourish in some truly great songs, firmly rooted in the popular tradition which Schumann himself had tried without notable success to cultivate. Meanwhile there was a more modest crop of folksong arrangements, again no doubt from sources found in Schumann's library. First came the *28 Deutsche Volkslieder* (not published until 1926), some of which were revised for the later collection of *49 Deutsche Volkslieder* of 1894; and then the 14 songs for children (*Volkskinderlieder*) dedicated to the family of Robert and Clara Schumann. This set, published anonymously in 1858, included the famous 'Sandmännchen' with its agreeable if overprettified verses and melody adapted from genuine folksong by Zuccalmaglio, and restored and preserved by Brahms's inspired accompaniment. The verbal picture is mere nursery-wallpaper; little flowers asleep in the moonlight, little heads nodding on tiny stems. But the added piano part embodies a real living tenderness for children asleep, just as in their father's song 'Der Sandmann' seven years before. Indeed, Brahms had become closer to the children than their father had been for some years before his breakdown. Brahms was more of an age, and less preoccupied. He was also very dear to their mother, whose absence on concert tours was hardly less enforced or permanent than her husband's. As Brahms's letters show, that absence had its proverbial effect. He must have been under intense and protracted emotional stress.

He later wryly compared his life from 1854 to 1856 with the plight of Goethe's romantic hero Werther, who killed himself for love of a married woman whose husband he admired. Brahms survived. But it may have given him some ironical amusement to reflect that Werther had sought relief from his intolerable bondage by taking an official position, for which he too was temperamentally ill-suited. However, such service meant more freedom for them both; and Brahms was certainly able to enlarge his social and musical horizons by moving, for three seasons, from Düsseldorf to Detmold, where he taught princesses and learnt from the court orchestra.

Song-writing was not among his duties; but Clara Schumann and her family still were. He had spent the summer of 1857 on holiday with them in Switzerland – an enchanted time of woodland walks and nightingales remembered in many a later song. But next summer Clara was staying with Brahms's friends the Grimms in Göttingen, where he later joined them; and there he met Agathe Siebold, the daughter of one of the university professors. She loved to sing, and Brahms to accompany her. They seemed made for each other; and certainly her gift for singing and affection inspired his genius for love-song. That summer they parted; and again her name and memory literally made music in his mind over the years. The radiant innocence of the fine 'Sonntag', Op. 47, no. 3 (1860), also seems to come from the remembered sunshine of July 1858. 'O liebliche Wangen', Op. 47, no. 4, though not published until 1868, sounds like the first and most naive of Brahms's many frankly sensual love-songs and would seem at first blush to have been meant for Agathe. 'Der Schmied' certainly was. Like 'Sonntag' it is a newly composed and unforgettable folksong melody; and its aural imagery adds a touch of new mastery. As the girl admires the strength and skill of her lover the blacksmith, the piano's sharply struck arpeggios ring and rebound in metallic brightness, partly in onomatopoeic imitation of hammer on anvil but partly also in a Brahmsian expression of personal pride in physical prowess, symbolised by the manual dexterity of hands on keyboard.

Another superlative song, 'Der Gang zum Liebchen', Op. 48, no. 1, belongs in style to this period, though published later – perhaps because the brilliant idea of weaving what is to become the postlude into the texture of the song itself may well (despite its natural and inevitable sound in the finished work) have taken a long time to devise and accomplish. Its subtle effect is to tincture an easy-going love-song with a drop of subtle sorrow. How absurd of her to fear that she might never see me again – how absurd of me to fear she may be unfaithful; thus the poem. But the music wistfully wonders why these thoughts should ever have occurred; and throughout the graceful dream and dance of the piano part those doubts persist in a gentle melancholy. The melody's last three notes and its arpeggio accompaniment resound in the songs of separation that were to follow. In these, as in the String Sextet, Brahms seems to use the notes A, G, A, H, E (cf. Ex. 5) to call her name and the notes A, D or A, D, E to pronounce or spell the word for 'farewell' in German.[1]

All those ideas may be heard in the two songs with linked musical and poetic themes, 'Scheiden und Meiden' and 'In der Ferne' (both 1858): and the latter's broken sixths like the sadly sighing breezes in Schubert's 'Der Lindenbaum' show that he, too, is far from forgotten. It is noteworthy also that Brahms turns instinctively to folksong when singing of his own lost love, as in

[1] 'Brahms's musical love-letters', *Musical Times,* April 1971.

'Trennung' and the early 'Ständchen' as well as 'Sehnsucht' (all 1858). The addition of Schubert to folksong provides the beautiful 'Vor dem Fenster' (also 1858), where the horn passages have the threefold symbolic function of evoking the rural scene, illustrating the watchman's horn, and recalling the music of Agathe's name. At the same time art-song is not forgotten. The Schubertian technique of moving between minor and major on the same tonic touchingly mingles moods of sadness and sweetness. Goethe's 'Trost in Tränen', already set by Schubert, is again chosen by Brahms, Op. 48, no. 5 (1858), with the same six-eight rhythm but without the same melodic inspiration. Clearly the poem, about the acceptance of grief and its consequent release, had some special meaning for him at that time. So too with the choice of a lyric in classical metre by Hölty (also a favourite poet of Schubert's), 'Der Kuss' (1858), which tells us more of the Agathe story in song-form. So does the music, the parallel sixths of which grace one of the contemporary folksong arrangements, 'Der Jäger', where also a young man loses his beloved and prays for solace.

The two worlds of courtly and popular tradition unite to give new scope to the music of 'Ein Sonett' (1858). The lyric is an old French troubadour lay translated by Herder in a book of folksong. Brahms matches the latter style with melody, the former with stately dance; and converts that unified meaning into one of his finest musical metaphors since 'Liebestreu'. 'Could I but forget her,' sighs the voice – and the piano's consecutive thirds move away down the keyboard, ready to sink into the desired oblivion – 'then I might find peace.' But 'alas, my heart remembers'. The thirds rise again, expand into sixths, grow into chords, filling all the stave and all the mind. Finally they grace the idea of 'schweben'. The lover and this thoughts hover around his lost lady, with a musical image of dancing courtly attendance, until the reprise of the melody turns to a sad ending, full of the unstilled longing of the flattened seventh (as in 'Vor dem Fenster').

Perhaps it was the idea of 'Ein Sonett' (a misnomer) which led to the search for an actual sonnet to set to music, and the discovery of 'Die Liebende schreibt' among the Schubert settings which Brahms was studying at this time. As it happened, that song and Mendelssohn's to the same text had recently been published. They both handle the doubly difficult form of combined sonnet and mono-logue with fine dexterity. But arguably Brahms surpasses them in his Op. 47, no. 5 (1858). His gently pleading sequences of melody, the illustration of 'weinen' by a two-note weeping motif which then (after a key-change to mark off the beginning of the sestet) is embodied in the vocal line in a more cheerful mood as the tears are dried; the division of the sestet by a questioning interlude to mark the interrogation in the text; the separation and recitative-like vocal inflexion of the last words: all these are eloquent of a master of song in its subtlest moods and forms. In a more personal way too this work is significant. So far the sad story of love and loss has been told in music from the man's point of view (which may suggest that two other songs on this theme to old German texts, 'Ich schell mein Horn ins Jammertal' and 'Vergangen ist mir Glück und Heil', are also 1858 farewells to Agathe, though not published for another ten years). But with 'Die Liebende schreibt' the perspective has changed, perhaps following the process already suggested in relation to Clara. Late in 1858 the song music seems to stop its own personal grieving. Instead it begins to offer conso-lation to girls who have lost their lovers.

This was always a strongly felt theme with Brahms; and the music continues to flow at deep levels. But it seems quite likely that he is becoming resigned to the loss of Agathe, and that his sentiments are turning to genuine remorse for any suffering or distress he may have caused her. 'Gold überwiegt die Liebe' usually ascribed to 1868, is a folksong in the 1858 style about a girl whose lover deserts her to make a rich marriage. One might again infer from Brahms's tendency to personal involvement with his song-texts, and from the comparative absence of musical interest as such, that this was somehow relevant to his separation from Agathe. He may have been reacting, for example, to the reproach that he valued his career more highly than marriage, as indeed he did; the richness of his art outweighed love.

The theme of deserted girls continues with 'Agnes', the setting of which in folksong style surely may well also date from 1858 (though usually ascribed to 1873). He was certainly reading Mörike at that time, as we know from his splendid setting of 'An eine Aeolsharfe', which brings the Agathe group to a fine close. This was surely the finest verse he had (or would) ever set to music. Musical recreation of poetry may not have been his gift; but this song has a stately beauty and dignity of its own. What may have begun as a personal valediction becomes an act of homage to lyric verse. The recitative alternating with melody, the mysterious harmonic changes at the invocation to the harp, its own dreamlike windblown strains in the typical left-hand arpeggios – all this, on a larger scale than anything Brahms had thus far achieved in song, must have given him new confidence in his constructional powers. He was ready for the song-cycle experiments which were to be his next major works in this form.

1861-69: Song Cycles

The *Magelone-Lieder*, like most of Brahms's more personal and domestic works, were surely conceived in the emotional environment of the Schumann household. He was always ready to provide and share songs and games and stories, no doubt including Ludwig Tieck's well-known *Novelle*, the full charm of which is conveyed only by its full title of *Liebesgeschichte der schönen Magelone und des Grafen Peter von Provence*. This is a French medieval tale translated into a German romance. That blend suited Brahms's taste (as we know from 'Ein Sonett'), so well that he set all but two of its interspersed lyrics to music as Op. 33. His settings freely repeat these already long poems, as if they were operatic arias; and this, surprisingly enough, is how Brahms imagined them.

In fact they are lyrical intermezzi, the technical purpose of which is to provide contemplative relief from the action and narrative detail of Count Peter's adventures. To see them so very differently Brahms must surely have been deep inside them, picturing himself as the hero. Indeed, there are very striking affinities. Count Peter, against his parents' wishes and to their distress, leaves home to seek his fortune, as Brahms had done. He is noted for his physical prowess, as Brahms was. He is inarticulate except when pouring out his heart in lyrics, when his self-expression suddenly becomes masterly. He has the knack of taking the wrong turning or doing the wrong thing, such as dozing off in moments of tension or crisis (as the young Brahms is endearingly said to have done during a performance, specially for him, of Liszt's B minor Sonata played by its composer). He is for much of his story a homeless wanderer or exile, as Brahms habitually thought of himself. He is often rejected because his undoubted merits and rank are unknown (a focal point of self-identification for the young artist). Above all, he has two loves, of comfort and despair. There is the virtuous and exalted Magelone, whom he manages to desert and abandon in a moment of confusion; and the exotic Sulima, to whose blandishments he nearly yields before escaping from her bondage and returning to his own true love. It was near enough to Brahms's own story to explain his choice of text. But his conscious task was to present a discursive short novel, full of incident and narration, in the *Lied* form; and this was hardly possible. If anyone could have succeeded, it was Schubert. Indeed, some of his early ballads (one might even instance his operas) achieve exactly that; and these are unmistakably the models for the *Magelone-Lieder*. The vocal melody provides the character and narration, while the piano part represents the action and scenery, unfolding and changing in leisurely panoramas as the story proceeds. The piano part is conceived as mere background to narrative and dramatic interest, of which there is no trace in the text. The music itself, however, is often admirable; and to any listener who can identify himself with Count Peter, as Brahms did, the experience will be illuminating. Thus construed, the songs are masterpieces; otherwise they tend to remain museum-pieces. The exceptions, understandably enough, are those that can be appreciated simply as lyrics without reference to their context, as in the delectable 'Ruhe, Süssliebchen' (1868) with its tenderness for a woman asleep, or the elegiac tones of 'Wie schnell verschwindet' (1868). But as a whole the *Magelone-Lieder* must regretfully be counted as failures in the attempted genre. A typical instance is the grand finale of the last song, 'Treue Liebe dauert lange' (1868). That theme of eternal love should have heralded a Brahmsian triumph. But the declamatory style is hardly ever on speaking terms with the shy and gentle lyrics.

This insoluble formal and stylistic contradiction may explain why these songs took ten years to complete, the last nine remaining unpublished until 1868-9. The contemporary work *Rinaldo* is another such confusion of genres, also no doubt undertaken because of a personal involvement with the text, this time by Goethe. Here, too, the hero is shown breaking free from the enchantment of a sorceress and returning to his own home. Again the subconscious mind is brooding on themes of chivalry and troth, of sacred and profane love.

It is reasonable to suppose that the same deep springs fed the notional song-cycle, Op. 32 (*c*. 1864), the work which Max Kalbeck, perhaps with the composer's own authority, described as 'Rinaldo caught again in the old toils'; it seems deliberately arranged to convey a story of lost love, remorse, and undying fidelity. This set – which was started later but finished much earlier than the *Magelone-Lieder* – is predictably more taut and concentrated in style. Instead of the eight-page *Gesang* changing its accompaniment-figures markedly, for narrative or dramatic purposes, every page or so, we now have a two-page *Lied* changing its accompaniment-style subtly, for lyric purposes, every few bars.

For a time both styles co-existed. They can be compared in two songs published in 1868, though no doubt both written earlier: 'Sehnsucht' (Wenzig) and 'Am Sonntag Morgen' (Heyse). Both are songs of longing and separation; both may be in memory of Agathe Siebold. The former is a lonely man's cry of yearning, in the spaciously dramatic *Magelone* style; the latter, a jilted girl's cry of grief, in the tauter and tenser lyric style of Op. 32.

This is to be the Brahms song-style from now on, as exemplified earlier (pp. 10–11). Its whole essence is condensed, concentrated, refined; and thus much more fully achieved and effective. It is as if some decisive turn of fortune *c*. 1862 (the year in which Brahms resolved to leave Germany and live in Vienna) had gone into the song-music and given it a final formulation. Sometimes the effort of concentration in both senses makes the music sound too thick or too cerebral. But generally it yields the perfect song-form, strong and substantial enough to bear the weight and tension of great thought and emotion. Essentially it is a variation-form in which given musical material is changed or inflected to match the words. Brahms rarely retains the same rhythm in the piano part, for example, for more than two or three bars at a time. But the fact is by no means obvious, because all the variations really restate the same basic theme. This is what gives his mature songs their own special quality of subtly brooding intensity. This is well exemplified by the songs of Op. 32 which focus on one or two images or rhymes at a time, in complete contrast with the diffuse style of Tieck. For this purpose the obvious choice was Platen, who was influenced by oriental verse-forms of this kind. Though a second-order poet, he was a fine craftsman. But Brahms is just as content with Daumer's clumsy imitations of the same style. He is concerned merely with a suitable basic form, which the music is to fill with personal lyric feeling. In the first song, Platen's sombrely impressive 'Wie rafft' ich mich auf', the rhymes recur on *Nacht, sacht, acht, gedacht* and so on, each a dark vowel sound with a hidden despondent 'ach'. The rhythms and accompaniment-figures in this song about sad walking at night change at every step; yet the beat persists as remorselessly as the rhyme. And all the changes are relevant to the words. Sometimes the connection is obvious; thus at 'the stars overhead' the arpeggios are made to radiate brightness and energy in the higher flights of the piano. But the symbolism is often as subtle and evocative as anything in the *Lied*. For example in this song the left-hand rhythms are gradually transformed, at the words 'the millstream pours through its rocky channel; I lean over the bridge', from powerful movement through a moment of poise to motionless contemplation:

Ex. 8

Throughout this cycle the poetry of music in motion recurs. In the second song, 'Nicht mehr zu dir zu gehen', the involuntarily returning footsteps in the bass line are heard belying the title. In the third the sidelong quavers underline the opening words 'Ich schleich umher'. The fourth, 'Der Strom, der neben mir verrauschte', travels with the moving stream of time; the fifth has a wild progression into the open air at 'hinaus in die Luft'. The seventh has a musical as well as a verbal metaphor of smooth sailing.

In the prelude of the last, the famous 'Wie bist du, meine Königin', two melodies move and sing together within the dream-world created by the left-hand arpeggios (much as in Ex. 4); the music is full of physical tenderness. Later, the minor semiquavers in an outlandish tonality wander dismayed through deserts of the musical imagination at the words 'durch tote Wüsten wandle hin'. Throughout Op. 32 even without the words we could hear the rhythms and tonalities walking in darkness or daylight, with lagging or lively steps.

The selection and arrangement of texts show that all this is for a woman's sake. The songs tell of lost time, wasted youth, deprivation of love, lack of fulfilment, bondage, depression and despair. They sing of one who is both ostensibly and truly sweet and saintly, yet who also sometimes seems bitter and resentful and unfair. Brahms surely had a real woman in mind and a real love at heart. In particular the music of the last song says, with total conviction and clarity, what Daumer's poor words can only stammer and mumble, namely (to borrow some better ones from Yeats)

> . . . up from my heart's root
> So great a sweetness flows
> I shake from head to foot.

Much of this music relates to his lifelong devotion to Clara Schumann, which dominates the songs from now on.

She was fourteen years older than Brahms. When they first met she was young, beautiful, and a supreme artist. Of course he fell in love with her. Soon he was writing music for her, including quotations from Beethoven's *An die ferne Geliebte*. One does not need to be a psychologist to understand this worship of a distant beloved. Brahms thought of Clara at a respectful, indeed reverential, distance; he dared approach her only through her husband as intermediary and intercessor. Schumann was like a dearly loved father; and Brahms's own father was seventeen years younger than his own mother. The difference in age may have made Clara Schumann all the more attractive and desirable; yet at the same time for the same reason all the more remote and forbidden. She was his ideal of all womanhood. 'Ask yourself,' he said to himself or wrote to his friends, when in doubt about any matter from morals to music, 'whether it would win the approval of a woman like Clara Schumann.' Thus she became a matron saint, as well as a passionately loved friend. No wonder their relationship both before and after Schumann's death was so fraught with frustration and tension; no wonder it led to quarrels and recriminations. Yet surely it taught Brahms all he knew of tenderness and compassion; and that experience was a main source of songs and other music for over forty richly productive years. 'I love you,' he told her in 1874, 'more than myself: more than anyone or anything in the world.' That feeling shines along every facet of the love-songs, lighting the sharp or smooth contours and colours of the music. Such music of course reflects a tenderness for other women: Agathe Siebold, Elisabeth von Stockhausen, Hermine Spies. But Clara outshone and outlasted them all.

1864-71: Love-Songs

This central phase is dominated by love-songs of all kinds. But however passionate the emotional expression, Brahms the musician

remains in conscious control. This is well illustrated not only by
'Die Mainacht' but also by the famous 'Von ewiger Liebe' (1864).
Even Hugo Wolf, rival song-writer and Brahms-hater, admired
this song for its symphonic breadth and intensity. It begins with a
typical musico-poetic image of two lovers walking through a wide
landscape of darkness, close together but isolated from the rest of
the world. In the poem their love is for some undefined reason
ill-fated, likely to evoke taunts and shame – a frequent theme in
Brahms. The choice of poem is also revealing.[1] It has been univer-
sally ascribed to Joseph Wenzig, although it is nowhere to be
found in the known source-books. It does, however, appear in the
poems of Hoffmann von Fallersleben in a volume known to have
been read by Schumann and presumably still in his library at
Düsseldorf during Brahms's sojourn there. The verses of ill-
omened yet enduring love may well have seemed especially relevant
in those years, and hence remained in his mind ready to turn into
music when the mood of darkness and disillusion again prevailed.
Meanwhile the contrasting mood of radiantly assured love had
already visited him at the time of his affection for Agathe Siebold,
and had then been expressed in the unpublished choral work
Brautgesang to words by Uhland. She and the song were both later
abandoned; but its opening melody (*a*) thriftily furnished the
protestations of undying love in 'Von ewiger Liebe' (*b*).

Ex. 9

(a)

Das Haus be - ne - dei' ich und preis' es laut, das empfang – en

hat ei - ne lieb - lich – e Braut

(b)

Eis - en und Stahl, man schmiedet sie um, un - se - re

Lie - be, wer wan – delt sie um?

[1] 'Zwei Brahms-Rätsel', *Österreichische Musikzeitschrift*, February 1972.

Similarly a pre-existing melody could easily explain why the word 'Mägdelein' has two different accentuations in two successive bars. Again, the horn passages in E minor clearly recall the Agathe songs of 1858. All these disparate feelings are built into one architectural design. First comes the wide-ranging darkness in the deep and broad bass melody, containing a progression in unison; two lovers walking in the night. Further, the two ideas are identified by the music itself: the opening vocal melody is the same as its accompaniment, the mood is as dark as the scene. The piano part becomes passionately insistent, the vocal line more declamatory, at the words 'leave me, sooner than suffer for my sake'. The music imagines a dramatic departure, driving onwards and away like wind and rain in the night (as the poem says) with a power not heard in the *Lied* since *Winterreise*. Then the mood moves into the major, to speak of eternal love. Here the music warms to its theme by illustrating the timeless and changeless nature of that vow. The same notes, the same phrases, the same figurations are repeated over and over again in the piano part until the total effect is finally rounded off and reinforced by a characteristic rhythmic shift as 3/4 time is broadened and strengthened into 3/2 to conclude the song.

An analogous recombining of emotion, allusion and reminiscence reappears in an even better-known work. In 1859 one of the members of the women's choir directed by Brahms in Hamburg was the seventeen-year-old Bertha Porubsky, who (knowing his penchant for popular melodies) sang him one from her native Vienna, the dialect ditty 'Du moanst (meinst) wohl, du glabst (glaubst) wohl'. Its burden was that love knows no law, and comes of its own sweet will or not at all. Brahms would have been inwardly impressed by that dictum – his own experience of love as of music – and he was openly enchanted by both song and singer. At the same time he had been reading the folksong collection *Des Knaben Wunderhorn*, where he would have found the little cradle-song beginning 'Guten Abend, gut' Nacht'. Meanwhile Bertha had returned to Vienna and married. In 1868 she had a new-born son. By then Brahms himself was a Viennese by adoption. In his mind the cradle-song and the love-song fused into what has become the world's best-loved lullaby – no doubt in response to the double share of affection it contains, in warm melody and rocking accompaniment, for both mother and child.

Brahms himself discerned this duality. Ex. 10 shows in simple
outline the complex process of welding two disparate melodic
ideas inseparably together by sheer technical brilliance and flair.

Ex. 10

Similar (if less conscious) work went into other Hölty songs
such as 'An die Nachtigall' (1868) with its melodic outlines softened
for the nightingale's song ('dein schmelzend Ach'), and with
quickening rhythms in the last page, this time in response to the
idea of flight ('Fleuch, Nachtigall . . .'). In 'An ein Veilchen' (1868)
the smooth spring of Schubertian water-music assumes a dark
velvety Brahmsian texture. Again its construction is like that of
'Die Mainacht' in its recitative elements and in the way in which
the whole weight of the music comes to rest dramatically on a
dominant seventh to draw attention to the reprise. 'If you see her,
tell her . . .' – what? asks the harmony; and with a quickening
rhythm the melody returns with the not unexpected but impressively
timed answer, 'Tell her that I weep for love of her'. In all these

Hölty songs the weighty and low-lying piano part expresses a search for deeper shadows, which sometimes attains profundity, sometimes obscurity. But this was always Brahms's way; he was at home in the depths of despair or the keyboard, in the warmth of love or of viola or contralto tones.

That penchant inclined him towards an instrumental style. In another Hölty song of this period, 'Die Schale der Vergessenheit' (1864), the music begins to take on that new turn. Its look on the page is that of a piano or violin sonata. Brahms felt perhaps that the classical metre and theme together, the plunging of love into the Lethean waters of oblivion, are not in themselves colourful or compelling enough for a viable song. So the music as such, not the song-form, is the primary impulse here. 'Die Kränze', too, also an exercise in classical prosody (though a much less adroit one, by Daumer) seems to have begun as instrumental music and then drifted into the song-form by way of a set of variations on the original theme. The combination of a piano piece with a poem about golden hair reminds us that in 1862 Brahms was giving piano lessons to the young Elisabeth von Stockhausen, who later married the composer Heinrich von Herzogenberg. We shall catch more glimpses of that golden hair in the last Brahms song about love, nearly thirty years later. He ended the lessons because he was falling hopelessly in love with her. Another man might have continued them for that reason. The disengagement tells us much about Brahms; and it may explain the comparative failure of 'Die Kränze', which despite its melodic charm is afflicted by the piano's curious inability to settle down to any one figure. This rhythmic restlessness seems to derive more from the composer's own state of mind than from any special relevance to the verses. Similarly in 'Liebesglut' (c.1868, also to words by Daumer, and again with a reference to waving tresses), the restlessness invades the tonality as well as the rhythm (remote flat keys are written in sharps, and conversely). The general effect is again that of a viola or clarinet sonata movement. In both songs the musical imagery (staccato for the falling of tears and the rising of dust) seems a little perfunctory, though such ideas are put to superlative uses in later songs. We feel also that Brahms is becoming more detached from his love-song texts, as if they were mere vehicles of his own emotions to be hailed and quitted at will.

In the *Liebeslieder-Walzer* (1868) for vocal quartet, also settings of Daumer, the ideas are literally detachable. In these masterpieces the piano duet accompaniments are so rich in contrapuntal detail and melodic and tonal invention that they can be played as separate works. The music is deeply serious but at the same time light and playful, combining vocal and instrumental genres in a technical and emotional *tour de force*. Another song from the same Daumer source-books, 'Botschaft' (1868), also contains effects similar to those in the earlier Hölty songs. For example the word 'sprich' (say) is repeated on a dominant seventh chord in order to herald and heighten the return of the main melody. The piano's thick-textured, heavily charged music needs a well-practised hand to keep it in check.

Between these settings and the earlier Daumer songs of Op. 32, sophistication has supervened. The verse is still at the same undemanding level; nothing has changed but Brahms. But he (at least in his songs) has become a different man, as if Vienna had realised a new potential. Of course the musical development is gradual. 'Magyarisch' (*c.* 1864) helps to define its nature, not only by its continued preoccupation with Daumer, the poetaster of eroticism, but by the knowing inflections of the vocal line. Here a touch of gipsy steals into the *Lied*. A lilt here, a cadence there, speak with a novel suavity. The musical phrase for 'eyes so dark yet so bright' sounds exactly like an elegantly well-turned compliment. Later Brahms went in quest of even lighter love-lyrics. 'O komme, holde Sommernacht' (1871) was dashing, even daring, for its day. Grohe's rather ineptly sensual text is glossed over in dazzling music full of Brahms's favourite student-serenade themes. There is a degree of academic ponderousness in the middle section, where the theme's announcement in left-hand octaves can easily sound contrived. But this impression is soon dispelled by the returning glitter of high black-key triplets, the dark and bright music made in Brahms's mind by a midsummer night and its dreams. Other indifferent but suggestive texts are given new life in the Kopisch songs. 'Die Spröde' (1871) is a sweetly Schubertian sigh of frustration. 'Blinde Kuh' (*c.* 1868) is a game of blind man's buff played on the keyboard. With a baffled touch in the harmonies, the playful fingers scurry around in dark and defeated quests before brightening in the hope of a major discovery. When Nietzsche complained of Brahms's impotence and Wolf of his inability to exult, they could not have known this and the other songs of Op. 58 (published in 1871), which are all virile élan. In 'Während des Regens' (*c.* 1868) the kisses fall and splash in a light shower of keyboard staccato. As we know from other music, including several later songs, the image of rain and tears and lost love was irresistibly vivid for Brahms. In this labile mood he was sure to think of Clara Schumann with all the old tenderness. Then the notes of levity are instantly replaced by those of the sternest gravity. Such a feeling of mixed solemnity and salacity clamours for more Daumer to plead its cause. In Op. 57 (1868) the sacred and the profane become bedfellows. The texts are frankly chosen to be as explicit as possible. 'Her eyes give me friendly looks; but love seeks more than this for its fulfilment, and that more is not vouchsafed'; thus no. 6. The entire opus is devoted to saying, in words and music, that she cannot really be as cold as (to the singer's sorrow) she seems; with such eyes, such breasts, it cannot be her nature.

It seems arguable, given the idea that Brahms used Schumann's Clara theme[1] as well as his own Agathe-theme, that the consistent relation of the former to exactly those features, in these songs as in others, is not mere coincidence. As Brahms told Clara, certain music made her physically present to him. He meant, I suggest, the theme which occurs in the Op. 57 songs whenever that physical presence is evoked. If so they speak for themselves, and – properly considered – with a profound power and pathos.

Ex. 11

(no. 7)

an ei – ne sol – che Brust

(no. 5)

an dei – ner Brust

(no. 6)

aus die – sem An – ge – sicht

(no. 6)

die – se Blick – e nicht

[1] *Musical Times*, May 1971.

(no. 4)

Ach, wen-de: die - sen Blick

This theme is discreetly threaded throughout; in its main B major form, for example, it appears in the opening vocal theme of no. 3, while in no. 7 it not only connects the prelude to the opening words 'The pearl necklace around your throat', but also provides the material which twice supports the opulent melodic curve of 'deiner schönen Brust' (at bars 14-15 and 18-19).

These are the songs which were criticised by some, solely on verbal grounds, as being over-erotic. But they are hardly that in any ordinary sense. They hymn a woman's breasts and eyes in a childlike appeal to mother-love. The theme recurs in a later song, 'Therese' (1878). Where the words speak of an appealing look in the eyes, the music makes a special excursion into B minor to find this same melody, e.g. at 'Was haben deine Augen für eine Frage getan?' Nor need we doubt at whose feet Brahms is sitting in still-poignant memory when he sings in his 'In Waldeseinsamkeit' (also 1878):

Ex. 12

Ich sass zu dein - en Füss - en

These quotations are given not solely to illustrate the nature of Brahms's feeling for Clara Schumann, but to make the more general point that his song-music is in every sense an embodiment of his emotions; and that these are not limited to a choice between grave or gay, epicene or erotic, but may well blend the two strains. Thus in 'Serenade', Op. 58, no. 8 (1871), a guitar-style accompaniment alternates with a langorous melody, like a mélange of a classical prelude, folksong and operetta. In 'Abenddämmerung' (1867) childhood memories and twilight dreams mingle with the shades of the departed. Thus filled with his own favourite feelings, Brahms brims with motivic ideas. The creeping semiquaver figures flow up like an incoming tide of darkness; the insistent bass pedal tolls like an evening angelus. Similarly in 'Herbstgefühl' (1867) we can hear that the words meant much to Brahms. Though not yet forty years old, he was audibly impressed with the unoriginal metaphor of the sere, the yellow leaf.

Ex. 13

All the music is made of images of separation. Even the two syl-
lables of the word 'welken' (wither) are sundered by a crotchet
rest, as if a leaf had just broken off. Most remarkable of all is the
peroration, which not content with echoing Schubert's *Winterreise*
almost quotes his 'Doppelgänger':

Ex. 14

(*a*) Schubert (transposed for comparison)

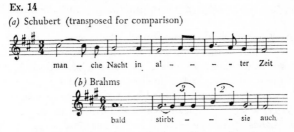

There is little doubt about the previous existence to which
Brahms's thoughts are now returning. At this time (1871) he also
set two poems by Hebbel. One, 'In der Gasse', Op. 58, no. 6, is
about the 'Doppelgänger' theme of revisiting the loved one's house,
now deserted, and standing outside alone. Another, 'Vorüber',
Op. 58, no. 7, is about a broken love-affair. Here, too, the music
takes the actual forms of the experience it embodies. Even the
accompaniment is distraught; the figures and ideas change more
hectically than ever. No doubt a memory of Clara was in mind; and
most of these sad solo songs, as we know from the letters, were
sent to her in manuscript. Her reaction was typical and delightful.
First she was profoundly moved by 'Abenddämmerung' and
'Herbstgefühl', which she could never read or play without tears –
understandably enough, since the desolate music of loneliness and
loss had sounded in her own mind for many a year. But that
grieving widowhood, together with constant worry about her
children, could only have enhanced her touching solicitude for
Brahms. 'Surely you are too young to write such music at your
age,' she writes. 'Marry some pretty girl; settle down.' As advice
to the greatest living song-writer it sounds absurdly Philistine. But
Clara's letters are to be read as if they were thoughts spoken

(sometimes outspoken) to the dearest of friends. In that context her advice may have been sound enough; and perhaps she was not wholly aware that she was herself a reason for not taking it.

The composer of all these songs of eternal fidelity was vowed to bachelorhood. But other songs suggest that he was far from vowed to chastity. If his loves were as clearly divisible as his works into sacred and profane, then his life if not indeed his music must have suffered from the resulting tensions. Some of that suffering is heard in the songs, together with a longing for release from strain and distress. 'Dämmerung senkte sich von oben' (1871), to words by Goethe, is a noble hymn to nightfall, in which the hurt gloom and confusion of minor key and wandering semiquavers is dispelled by a cool healing moonrise. This theme of tension and release will recur often from now on. In several songs a moonrise or a cool wind comes to heal and refresh the hurt mind. And here the lulling rhythms and relaxing harmonies foretell the end of 'Ich wandte mich', the second of the *Four Serious Songs* of nearly thirty years later, where they mean a calm and easeful death.

The shades gather closer still in 'Schwermut', Op. 58, no. 5 (1871). The inner voices of this slow choric lament are the singer's own requiem. The mood of this phase hovers between Keats and Shelley; from being half in love with easeful death to lying down like a tired child and weeping away this life of care. As the text of 'Schwermut' says, 'I am burdened with thought, tired of life; let me lay my head down in the night of nights.' The verses, hopeless in every sense, are by Carl Candidus, a very minor poet already set by the ailing Schumann. No doubt the volume came, like many another, from the Düsseldorf library and the mood from the Düsseldorf days. It is expressed by the mature Brahms in music of great power. The piano part concentrates on two basic rhythms – insistent minims for sorrow, off-beat minims for sleep, symbolising the presence or absence of stress. But in this mood the songwriting impulse itself sleeps or dies.

1873-74 and 1875-78: Memories and Nostalgia

Between 1871 and 1873 the field of song lay fallow. Brahms had other work on hand, and was content to link his occasional reading with his perpetual music-making whenever a poem or a woman caught his fancy. And for friendship's sake he was usually ready to respond to a personal request or commission.

Thus when in 1873 Olga Precheisen was playing Ophelia, and wanted new settings of the English texts, Brahms obliged with sketched melodies and piano accompaniments (first published in 1935). His willingness to provide them is almost the only interest they have. Much the same applies to Gottfried Keller's request for a setting of some verses written for a friend's wedding. Brahms was again ready to oblige with the forgotten 'Kleine Hochzeits-kantate' (1874). Much more personal and compelling was an appeal from Clara Schumann for him to look at some poems written by her son (also his godson), the unhappy Felix, who at seventeen was already infected by a fatal tuberculosis. His verses, though clumsy and naive, are full of a promise which could never be fulfilled. Brahms must have found them indescribably touching in their naive and helpless craving for life and love. 'Meine Liebe ist grün' (1873) enshrines devotion to Clara, pity for her sick son and reverence for her dead husband; and it also contains Brahms's own unfeigned pleasure in love-song lyrics decorated with lilacs and nightingales. His music is tender and hopeful; its characteristically complex message is conveyed by reference to Schumann's 'Schöne Fremde' (compare the postludes of each) about great joy in store.

The gift proved therapeutic. 'How beautiful the song is!' wrote Clara in heartfelt gratitude; 'its postlude alone is something I could go on playing for ever. . . We said nothing to Felix, and in the evening Joachim came, and I showed it to him, and we began to play it through.' Then up came Felix, and elicited that this beautiful piece was the latest Brahms song. So of course 'he asked whose the words were; and when he saw they were his own he went quite white'. Another of his texts appears in 'Wenn um den Hollunder' (1874), which at least shows what a great composer can do by sheer mastery of invention and organisation. It too might well have been played by Joachim and Clara as a work for violin and piano. So might some of the other love-songs completed in 1873–4, including Brahms's first settings of poems by his friend Klaus Groth.

So far as is known, they were not commissioned. Brahms responded to them as poetry. Yet there is in the music a certain reserve, as if this were his governing mood at the time. In 'Mein wundes Herz' (1873) the hurt heart is less evident than the contra-puntal brain. The expressively wide-ranging melodic line becomes first, in diminution, the right-hand accompaniment figure and then, in imitation, its bass:

Ex. 15

'Dein blaues Auge' (1873) has a deceptive plainness and simplicity. 'How blue your eyes, how healing after those other eyes whose memory haunts and hurts me still: deep blue and cool as a lake.' These are sentiments suitable for inward contemplation rather than direct expression. The song too is still and cool on the surface, with a stately melody as placid and pellucid as lake-water. Its form is clearly contrived as A B A surrounded by prelude and postlude. But at the very centre there is a moment of troubled turbulence in the harmony, a hint of pangs persisting despite all the healing of time. The same scene reappears in 'Auf dem See' (1873), to words by Carl Simrock. Music and musician alike turn to nature for comfort and inspiration. The wave-motion in the piano part is a soothing lullaby; the poem's compact imagery of refreshing coolness and beauty – snow-capped mountain, cool water and the reflection of one in the other – is turned into slow assuaging music. As the last verse says, 'so we should reflect in our songs all the loveliness of the world'; it might have served as a motto for all Brahms's songs of this period. We can imagine how in this mood he scanned other volumes of verse for suitable texts, in a subconscious search for mood-pictures to paint, showing far-away scenes or faces from long ago. In 'An ein Bild' (1874), to a poem by Max von Schenkendorf, the frame is both square and ornate. The opening vocal melody may recall Agathe (cf. Ex. 5). Certainly the words are about taking the well-known road to her house, the 'Doppelgänger' motif. The poem alludes once again to the soothing effect of contemplating the deep sea, or a remote star; and the musical response is analogous to 'Auf dem See' in its deep pedal notes, reiterated rhythms, and alternations between left hand and right. 'Erinnerung' (1874), also to words by Schenkendorf, is especially fine. Its broad, seemingly endless melody is a floodtide of sighs flowing all the way back to a vanished past, rejuvenating old memories into new life. The rondo form also has variations fitted to the sense of the words. The rhythmic patterns grow steadily more active and varied as the images of remembered life and love become more vivid in the mind. Then the last verse resumes the leisurely pace of the first, to show that the original mood of reverie is resumed as the pictures from the past finally fade.

This nostalgia dominates Brahms's song-writing at this period; the withdrawal from present reality into childhood and nature goes almost to vanishing point. For this mood, Klaus Groth was the right poet. He was not only a personal friend of Brahms but came from the same part of Germany; they both remembered the same boyhood. His best-known work is in North German dialect, which Brahms revealingly said was too *personal* a language to set to music. Two poems, 'Regenlied' and 'Nachklang' (both 1873), are linked by the same musical image of rain. The separate staccato drops of 'Während des Regens' run together in flowing melody and accompaniment quavers. At the same time the recurrent rhythm suggests both interruption and flow, drop and trickle. All this insistent imagery conceals the essential difference in style of the two poems, which are subordinated to the composer's needs. In 'Regenlied', old memories reawaken refreshed like flowers after rain. 'Nachklang' is metaphysical: it compares rain with tears. Brahms was impressed by this image: it was the only poem for which he ever provided two different solo settings. The earlier version (c. 1866) remained unpublished until 1908. It too has the staccato which meant drops of rain or tears to Brahms. But the later setting's rhythm and melody are an overflow from 'Regenlied' with its evocative first line 'Walle, Regen, walle nieder'. In the music all these notions flow into one: the feeling is that rain is nature's means of relief and release as tears and memories are ours. The pictures of boyhood bathing and paddling are painted in bold splashes of sound. But the first lyric is too long and gushing, and the distended middle section sags sadly. The second is more reflective, with poignant clash chords as the harmonies are forced together by a concentration of sad thoughts; but even there the words chafe and drag. The music really comes into its own as the finale of the G major Violin Sonata of 1875. Meanwhile in 1874 Brahms continued his fervent retrospection with three more Groth poems specially selected and grouped like a family album, a triptych of nostalgia. 'Regenlied' recalled a lost boyhood happily enough: but 'O wüsst' ich doch den Weg zurück' broods over it, mourns and grieves for it. Brahms had passed his fortieth year; and his mood was approaching self-pity. Phrases like 'zum zweitenmal ein Kind' could so easily have sounded like a second childhood in quite the wrong sense. Instead, his music has a nobility and grandeur which entirely transforms this feeling and transcends the poem. The great waves of arpeggios dream and sigh like a whole ocean of regret and longing for the past. The music is also serene in its acknowledgment that real life knows no return. At 'vergebens such' ich nach dem Glück' we hear the vain search for happiness in the ominous octaves which to Brahms meant not only desolation but dissolution. The poet's feeble cliché of 'ringsum ist öder Strand' becomes the barren shore of a darker sea, an image of grave Tennysonian beauty.

Both the other songs of this trio seem to pass beyond this world. Their nostalgia invokes not only early life but early death. 'Wie traulich war das Fleckchen' makes its musical imagery from the ideas of a rocking cradle and a far-off dream; and the harmonies of rest and repose, as discords are eased back on to the tonic, foretell the final resolutions of the *Four Serious Songs*. Again, in the third song, 'Ich sah als Knabe', the idea of lost youth seems to remind Brahms of Schubert's sweetly resigned 'Zügenglöcklein' (The Passing Bell). The passing of youth in poetry becomes the passing of life itself in music. Similarly in 'Frühlingstrost' (1874), the first of two songs to words by Schenkendorf, we hear the regretful sighs of remembered serenades from an earlier spring-

42

time, arranged in the formal patterns characteristic of this song-writing period. 'An die Tauben' (1874) shakes free of these obsessions. The typical minor-Romantic idea of love's greeting tastefully conveyed by carrier-pigeon (as in Schubert's 'Die Taubenpost', Schumann's 'Aufträge') inspires the most graceful of melodic flights. Even a final reference to death, which Brahms might well have been expected to linger over, is brushed aside by the winging music. The success of this amorous mood may have inspired the choice of another would-be erotic Daumer lyric. The inept text of 'Eine gute, gute Nacht' winks and leers. 'You wish me a good night; if you really wished me one you could make it so.' But Brahms in this mood of restraint and humility makes the point by a self-effacing diminution:

Ex. 16

It is as if even this one love-song of 1873-4 shrinks from actual touch. All the rest is picture, distance, perspective, broadening out into great vistas of time and space, life and death. If this objective phase could be fired by some truly personal emotion the result would surely be a series of great songs.

Again there was a fallow period. But Brahms's roots remained receptive to rain-symbolism, as in the 'Regenlieder'. This, and his friendship with Keller, may have predisposed him to set 'Abendregen' (1875), which begins with a light soothing shower in staccato quaver chords. More important perhaps was an element of personal response, not to a real request but to a fancied rebuke. In 1875 Wagner sought the return of a *Tannhäuser* manuscript which had come into Brahms's possession. Neither was to blame; there were no recriminations. Yet Brahms seems to have felt his integrity impugned; and perhaps he sought consolation in song. The poem envisages immortality for the artist, who in ages to come will see not merely his name unsullied but his head inaureoled. But the promised rainbow sounds over-arch in its colourful solemnity.

Clara Schumann rejected the resulting song, tactfully blaming the rather pompous poem. Brahms was really too modest a man to preach a sermon on the text of his own immortality; and his music, which would have been admirable as an instrumental work, is uneasy in the *Lied* form. The same applies to Felix Schumann's 'Versunken' (1878), where a jejune image of being engulfed in an ocean of love is treated with almost cerebral detachment in the two-to-one relation of accompaniment figure to vocal line:

Ex. 17

The music could rarely grow from the deepest levels unless the words had first worked their way into Brahms's emotional life and put down roots there. Then they could be quick to germinate, if not to flower. This, the composer's own metaphor, can again be exemplified by an occasional song. It was in 1874 that Brahms first met Max Kalbeck, whose lifelong devotion later expressed itself in the best-documented biography. Brahms in turn took a benevolent interest in the young man's unpublished verses. He was straightaway sent some manuscript poems, including the text of 'Nachtwandler' (Sleepwalker). The song is known to have been in essence complete by 1877. But not even its poet was allowed to see or hear it until 1882, when it was at last ready for publication as Op. 86, no. 3. Its perfectly wrought music is full of intense feeling, like moments of fire within years of refining. This goldsmith solicitude for the finish of the art-work is touching and revealing. Clearly it puts a further gloss on the processes and time-scale of the songs. But it also throws light on the creative idea. The palpable inspiration must derive from the central image of the lover as sleepwalker blissfully skirting precipices, without harm to himself or others as long as he is not brought to his senses, but dangerous if aroused. This much was apparent to Elisabeth von Herzogenberg, who described the verses as 'far from edifying'. Max Kalbeck himself agreed; and added revealingly that their emotional content exactly fitted the frame of mind in which Brahms found himself at the time.

The song's assured yet tranced movement, its melodic unisons with the voice expressing isolation, its languishing alternations of major and minor thirds are all enriched in the last verse by the addition of deep bass notes, obsessive syncopations, and contrary motion between voice and piano – a beautiful expression of the subconscious mind and its powerful stream of impulse running strongly counter to surface appearance.

Such a surge of new power in response to a rather insignificant poem must have made Brahms aware of a new stage in his development as a song-writer. This may explain why, quite exceptionally, he dated his next four songs (all in May 1876) as if they marked some mile-stone. All four respond not only to motives of personal feelings of friendship or love, but also to the actual words of the chosen texts. Typically, these are divided between the poetic extremes of Goethe and Candidus.

Each setting is in a sense dramatic. Goethe's 'Serenade' comes from a play. The song, like the lyric, is apparently a mere trifle, which on analysis proves unexpectedly complex and deep. 'Why do lovers torment and deceive themselves; why do they feel that happiness is to be found only where they are not? Tell me that, sweet child.' It is a song of the subconscious. The question is lightly posed, but the answer sounds out the depths and shoals of human nature. So the melody sighs and smiles, while the accompaniment weighs and reflects – in ponderous bass notes and canonic imitation.

'Unüberwindlich' is a racy Goethe lyric full of broad but deft humour. It compares women with wine – alike in being irresistible, beneficial when taken in moderation, but stupefying if indulged in to excess. Again the music acts and mimes, in portly octaves and sparkling acciaccature, with a sprightly popping of corks and corsages. The portentous speech of slur and hiccup is hit off as neatly as anything in the *Lied*. And Brahms even adds a novel quasi-verbal device, by beginning with four staccato bars of Domenico Scarlatti like a dry and sparkling wine. The piece quoted appeared in a volume of two hundred reviewed by Schumann in the *Neue Zeitschrift für Musik* in 1839, with the comment that so large a collection should be taken in moderation. So Brahms's brief sample, like his whole sparkling song, may well have been intended to apply to both cases, women as well as wine.[1]

The two Candidus songs paint a darker picture. In 'Sommerfäden' confused thoughts of love drift like gossamer (of an unusually tough and durable Brahmsian variety). This musical image of dark bewilderment quite eclipses the already rather dim verses. 'Alte Liebe', too, is redeemed from its witless words by the controlled passion of the music. The poet feels that he is being tapped gently on the shoulder by a visitation from the past, accompanied by an odour of jasmine for which he is at a loss to account. From this unpromising situation Brahms conjures a frail and tender ghost of lost love, a wistful and elusive fragrance. Perhaps it is not coincidence that the music has at that moment an air of Clara (the left-hand melody) to whom the song was sent almost as soon as written. 'Im Garten am Seegestade' (1877), to verses by Lemcke, also has those themes in the vocal line at the concluding words about lost love and endless longing. The walk in the wood described in 'Im Waldeseinsamkeit' (1878) with its revealing opening melody (Ex. 12) brings to life the pictures and pressed flowers of Clara Schumann's album in which she wrote 'Flowers picked for Johannes', 'Enchanted evening walk with Johannes' and so on. Lemcke's inept words stress the note of sentimental keepsake. But the music still flowers in the Brahms song-album, preserved by his evident sincerity and mastery. The final notes of the nightingale resound from his memories into those of his listeners in perpetuity.

That yearning alternation of B major and minor is also heard in the beautiful 'An den Mond' (1877), another song of sleepless nights, separation, sad slow walking under the moon. Again the text was surely selected (this time from Simrock's poems) for those evocative ideas. So was the Brentano poem 'O kühler Wald' (1877), with its irresistible theme of 'In what wood now does my love go walking? Where now is the echo of my songs? In no wood now, in no real world, but in my heart for ever'. The slow Tristan-esque movement of repeated crotchet chords is made to spread apart and rustle in separate quavers, as the forest stirs in the memory; while at the heart of the song are the longest, slowest and softest chords of all, their pulse serene and assured to match the words 'Im Herzen tief'. Again the gravity and restraint of the music avoid all sentimentality; and the clear personal feeling adds real poignancy.

[1] 'Zwei Brahms-Rätsel', *Österreichische Musikzeitschrift*, February 1972.

In the Candidus 'Geheimnis' (1877), melodic grace again redeems maudlin verse. The trees rustle in a spring twilight of quiet arpeggios. These keyboard echoes of 'Im Garten am Seegestade' together with the vocal echoes of 'Alte Liebe' suggest that all these songs were born of the same inspiration. Further heights are reached with 'Lerchengesang' (1877), also by Candidus, where the distant trill of dawn larks aloft evokes memories as tender as any twilit nightingale. The idea of open spaces inhabited solely by falling melody is translated into song with Wolfian mastery by the use of wide intervals in the piano followed by unaccompanied vocal lines; even the look of the music on the page suggests a high singing in empty air.

Brahms had by now become a great song-writer in the definitive sense of writing music which is framed to the life of the words. As always this genre puzzles the pure musician, for example Clara Schumann. She complained about the Hölty 'Minnelied' that the contrasting section at the words 'without her, all is dead, the very flowers are withered' lacked melodic interest. So in a sense it does. No doubt Brahms at one time shared her uncertainty; and this could have delayed till 1877 his completion of the song, which may well have been conceived ten years earlier with the other Hölty settings. But the practised song-writer sees that the idea of 'lacking interest' was precisely what had to be expressed in a musical metaphor which must not itself be uninteresting. The aim is perfectly achieved with little bursts of canon heralding the triumphant return of the grand main tune.

Meanwhile the personal emotive pattern persists as before. Hand in hand with the music of courtly love, grave or gay, go some very worldly songs, with their concomitant mood of withdrawal into disillusion, and longing for the healing forces of nature or of death. But now all the underground streams and sources of feeling are running and cascading together in the musical mind. Love blends into nature, which in turn merges into the natural expressions of folksong by gradual transition. Thus 'Tambourliedchen' (1877) sounds both cheerful and popular. Clara found it 'too Schubertian', meaning no doubt the piano-sonata style of the accompaniment. But it at least showed how, treated with added sophistication, the substratum of popular song could still prove fertile. Light music and light love soar together in the ingratiating high spirits of 'Es liebt sich so lieblich im Lenze' (1877), the first of six Heine settings.

In 'Willst du dass ich geh'?' (1877) the eroticism in meaning and music is even more lightly clad. 'Must I go? Must I leave you – on so dark and cold a night?' A leading question; and we may agree with Elisabeth von Herzogenberg that Lemcke was not the man to ask it. But Brahms was; the music is piercingly sweet in its cry of longing, involved in every sense with its hidden melodies inflected by dominant harmony into one intense question-mark. The major resolution of the final loud chord may suggest that the lover is after all allowed to stay on the desired side of the shut door. If so, it was for the last time, even in the imagination. From now on, the feeling of being left outside in the cold becomes increasingly intense in the choice and treatment of Brahms's song-themes, for example in 'Über die Heide' (*c.* 1877), sadly his only setting of the excellent poet Theodor Storm. Again the lyric is clearly chosen from a wide reading to correspond with the composer's mood, always achingly sensitive to any touch on the 'Dopplegänger' theme of revisiting the past. The idea of footfalls on a deserted moor resounds in hollow echoing octaves. The sad memory of past happiness is recalled by the sad melody of an earlier love-song of 1864, 'Wehe, so willst du mich wieder' (piano left hand):

Ex. 18

Über die Heide

Lie – be, wie flog es vor – bei!

Wehe, so willst du mich wieder

Into 'Verzagen' (1877), in accents unheard since the ocean's raging in 'Verzweiflung', from the *Magelone-Lieder*, Brahms pours the blind fury of winds and waves, drowning Lemcke's feeble poem in a real despair. But although the words attempt a virile defiance, the music is resigned; the voice is borne helplessly along on a surge and swell of demisemiquaver arpeggios. These dark tides of fate are not only welcomed but embarked upon in the spiritless 'Todessehnen' (1878), to a poem by Schenkendorf, where the longing for death is imagined as a healing wind, playing from the grave across the brow. This feeling infiltrates the masterly 'Feldeinsamkeit' (*c.* 1878), where the experience of lying idly alone

in a meadow, watching the clouds and drifting away v
is marvellously imagined in music. The motionless ba
of terra firma are overshadowed by high chords where
voices ceaselessly shift and blend without changing their s
like moving cloud-shapes. But the idea of leaving the world behind
becomes so powerful that when the words say, innocuously
enough, 'It is as if I had long since passed away', sombre octaves
suddenly put on deep mourning. The poet, Hermann Allmers, was
quite right to say that the music went far beyond his words; only
that transcendence keeps his name alive.

When nature remains planted on this earth, the music is less
blissful. 'Frühlingslied' (also 1878) hardly leaves the ground. The
rejuvenating effect of springtime is invoked in the words, but not
the music, which contains no new invention except the rising
seventh with which the vocal line begins, perhaps in response to the
word 'geheimnisvoll' (mysteriously). Two other contemporary
spring songs to words by Geibel were stillborn; even this one has
scarcely survived. But the magic returns when nature symbolises
the mystery of human feeling. This happens by design in two
Heine settings (both 1878), 'Sommerabend' and 'Mondenschein',
where Brahms again forces two poems into the same music in
order to impose his own interpretation on the words. Both songs
unite two very typical ideas; walking disconsolate at night, and
then being assuaged by a romantic vision whether of watersprites
bathing in streams or the landscape bathed in moonlight. The
second song begins with the ominous octaves already noted in
'Feldeinsamkeit', for the words 'night lay upon the dark roads':

Ex. 19

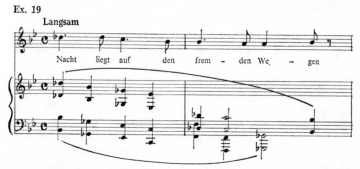

Then a flood of mellowness wells into the music. All stresses and accents are removed or elided, as in earlier songs about the melting strains of nightingales. The vocal line and piano melody vie together in the arpeggios which meant contentment to Brahms. The same music is used in the earlier song to illustrate golden moonlight in a dark blue sky. Each passage sounds like a love-song; and blue and gold were (as we know from the letters) the dress and colouring of Elisabeth von Herzogenberg. Other songs with words about nymphs bathing in moonlight were also sketched in secret homage to her. Brahms had already taken flight from her as from Agathe. But long after he had stopped leaving girls, or even finding them, the ideas and moods of their love-longing and desertion lingered obsessively in his mind. In earlier years it had seemed that he was concerned first with his own grief and later with theirs; and then the mood passed, often yielding to levity or disillusion. In 1877-8 it recurs with immense force, as if all the love-songs for Clara and others had aroused dormant memories even more poignant and disturbing than ever. The sad picture of the deserted girl goes naturally into the folksong frame: and Brahms was by now a practised artist in the song-form. So the folksongs of this period have two aspects. They are advanced in technique, yet retreat into a vanished past. Even the choice of words reflects this dichotomy: the poems are usually not folksong as such but German translations of popular Czech or Serbian songs. 'Klage II' ('O Felsen, lieber Felsen', 1877) is clearly related musically to a folksong arrangement (no. 38 of the *49 Deutsche Volkslieder*), the words of which had already been used in an original setting ('Gang zur Liebsten') of nearly twenty years earlier. 'Vom Strande' (1877), the folksong origins of which are overlaid but not concealed by the complex and elaborate piano part, is a setting of Eichendorff, whose verses had not been used in a solo song for more than twenty years. The combination of art and folk, experience and innocence, sounds like the mating of naive young melodies with old and knowing accompaniments, e.g. in 'Klage I' and 'Mädchenlied' (1878): as also later in 'Das Mädchen' (1884) where the mating of youth and age is the actual theme. Parental voices prophesying doom or offering counsel also reappear in the songs after twenty years; thus a new voice is added in the piano part of 'Des Liebsten Schwur' (1877), when father's warning tones are heard in the imagination. The piano part has hidden felicities matching the delighted secrets hinted at by the voice. First the subdominant and then its own subdominant express the idea of complete submission, which is amusingly contradicted by the offbeat accents and the easy assurance of the rhythms at the end of each verse.

Brahms's folksong expression quite often wears an endearing smile. Just as it was easier for him personally to relax in the country, so it was easier for his music to relax in the pastoral convention. But even there, and even in the falsetto of the women's songs, the voice remains clearly his own in its mature blend of textual richness and melodic simplicity, and its themes of separation and farewell. 'Ade!' (*c.* 1877) well illustrates all these aspects; it is worth comparing with Robert Franz's sweetly bland setting of the same text. 'Abschied' and 'Über die See' (both 1877) are also typical. Again, both recall earlier days; the former in its Schumannian style and the latter in its affinity in key and melody with the Agathe songs of 1858.

The essential identity of art song and folksong in this period can be judged from 'Mädchenfluch' and 'Salome' (both 1877). In each Brahms shows his empathy into the feelings of women sundered from their lovers. The former is a translation, presumably of a genuine Czech folk poem: the latter is a setting of a sophisticated and stylised poem by Gottfried Keller. Yet the two songs are similar in their blend of free-flowing melody and artificial accompaniment. In each the vocal line stretches the rhythm and sense of the words to breaking point, a fact which Hugo Wolf was quick to notice in the Keller song. He himself set the same poem, so that his mind's already acute critical edge was fine-honed by rivalry. In a letter he quoted the Brahms tune:

Ex. 20

and added scornfully 'so it yodels along to the end, in the well-known folksong strain'. He would have agreed that a veil is best drawn over 'Salome'. But its companion piece 'Therese' (1878), also to a poem by Keller, is much more mysterious and seductive. Clearly the verses made a very deep impression on Brahms (and on Wolf, whose own setting makes an illuminating contrast) for reasons clarified by the text, in which a mature woman says to a very young man, 'Why do you look at me so? All the wise men in the world would be baffled by the question in your eyes. But there's a sea-shell on the mantelpiece: just put your ear to that'.

Again, the text has a folksong style. Keller is known as a tenderly sympathetic observer of the rural scene in many a poem and short story; and his later revision of these verses deliberately places the encounter out of doors, even at the cost of transforming the sea-shell into a snail-shell with a consequent loss of poetic reverberations. The original version conveys more powerfully the sense of the mystery of nature which, as we have seen, moved Brahms profoundly in these years. Wolf's curious snail-shell whisperings are as nothing compared with the booming of Brahms, in whose mind the sea is sounding in all its mysterious solemnity. In this deeply felt masterpiece, gravity of feeling and lightness of touch attain a lasting poise. With 'Therese' the song-music achieves a well-rounded and mature wisdom which it maintains to the end.

1881-84 and 1885-86: Resignation and Serenity

As before, a period of silence in song-writing seems to have been broken by a personal appeal: and the themes to which Brahms reverts are those of art and folk, youth and age. Hans Schmidt, at one time tutor to the Joachim children, was among the young men encouraged by Brahms to write and send verses. Those chosen for immediate setting in Op. 74 ('Sommerabend', 'Der Kranz', 'In den Beeren', all c. 1882) seem entirely unremarkable save in taking the form of an imagined dialogue between mother and daughter, a dramatic idea which played a vital part in the Brahmsian fantasy-life. 'Der Kranz' even repeats exactly the same poetic theme as 'Liebestreu' of twenty years earlier; mother advises daughter to forget the unfaithful young man, but love cannot be so lightly set aside. Parental advice and comment, and especially the mother-child relation, always form one focus of the song music. Among the great thoughts which the young Brahms earnestly transcribed into a note-book was this gem – 'Only one thing on earth is better and more beautiful than a wife – a mother'. It reads as if the difference were only one of degree, and not even a prohibited degree at that. As we have seen, Brahms himself was fourteen years younger than his revered mother-figure Clara Schumann; his own father had been seventeen years younger than his mother. He had found no incongruity in combining a cradle-song for a child with a love-song for its mother, as in 'Wiegenlied' (Ex. 10). He idolised children and he idealised childhood. All the women he loved were musicians, and most were singers. So we can imagine the tenderness he would have felt when in 1863 his dear friend Joachim became engaged to the contralto Amalie Schneeweiss. Of course he stood godfather to their first-born – the son of Joseph, baptised through Johannes, born to a mother whose name (white as snow) symbolised virginity, and who sang divinely. In such a ceremony of love and reverence his creative mind turned to a contemplation of the old lullaby folksong-carol 'Joseph, lieber Joseph mein'. Over the next twenty years, further ideas were added; first a reading of Lope da Vega's 'Cradlesong of the Virgin', in Geibel's translation, and secondly the metamorphosis of a warm maternal voice into the sound of a viola obbligato. In the song 'Geistliches Wiegenlied', completed in 1884, the viola sings its traditional lullaby, while the voice calls upon the night-winds of Bethlehem to be calm and warm, not to wake or chill the sleeping child. Art-song and folk-song are blissfully at one.

Hugo Wolf's superlative setting of the same text creates a moving picture of wind-blown tree-tops. Brahms paints in his warmest coloured harmonies a static tableau of mother and child; his music is all song and slumber with parallel thirds and rocking rhythms that recall the lullaby love-song 'Ruhe, Süssliebchen'. The winds sometimes sing and sigh in sympathy; they never threaten or disturb. When the poem foreshadows a greater anguish to come, the music is content with a touch of solemnity in a rather per-functory change to the tonic minor. But this momentary coldness offers a fine formal contrast to the final return of the singing themes, warmly at ease as before. At this time when Brahms was pouring out twenty years of love and wisdom in music for voice and viola, he was fortunate enough to find, in Rückert's 'Gestillte Sehnsucht' (1884), another poem where the same symbolism was valid. 'Winds sing the world to sleep; what will sing me to sleep? Only death.' This time the text (with one verse omitted) fits fairly if squarely into the prepared A B A frame. The solo viola again becomes a symbol of singing. But this time it is the lullaby sound of mother nature herself, with the wide-ranging Brahmsian arpeggios that embrace a whole imagery of sighing winds, singing birds, and the gamut of human yearning making music until the night comes. No richer sounds of sunset had ever been heard in music.

The mellow D major, and the elegiac moods of submission to love and fate, simultaneously *Requiem* and *Liebeslied*, recur just as memorably in 'Sapphische Ode', no. 4 of Op. 94 (published in 1884), to another poem by Hans Schmidt which in itself is merely a modest and euphonious blend of Greek metre with German rhyme. But the luscious central image of a love like roses whence tears of joy drop like dew moves Brahms into a sensuous beauty of melodic line, worthy of his contemporary Violin Concerto. The detached drops of staccato, the melodic echoes of Schubert's Heine setting 'Am Meer', are alike shared with the *adagio* of the Piano Trio, Op. 8, in its first (1854) version, which was written in homage to Clara Schumann: and the song sounds as if drawn from the same memories, though riper and sweeter by many years. A sad Heine seascape reappears in 'Meerfahrt' (*c.* 1884), where the lovers row past in silence on a comfortless sea to the strains of a lugubrious barcarolle. The woodland walk (as in 'Waldeseinsamkeit') is relived in the gentle strolling measures of 'Wir wandelten' (*c.* 1884), to a poem by Daumer in which tender thoughts sentimentally peal like golden bells. Brahms's musical response chimes high in the keyboard with so striking a felicity that the flaw of falsity vanishes and the music rings true.

All these blue and green seascapes and landscapes in music seem to depict scenes with Clara. B major and minor had been especially redolent of her ever since her husband had written the *Davidsbündler* for her – 'wedding thoughts', as he called them. Brahms once said that her eyes looked out at him from that music (cf. also Ex. 11). Now in the same key to similar themes Brahms sets 'Beim Abschied', no. 3 of Op. 95 (published in 1884), a valedictory poem by Friedrich Halm. 'I don't really care for the men friends in my circle; they may stay or go, just as they please. But I do care for the one woman for whose sake I endured them all; and now I am to lose her.' This obscure utterance clearly moved Brahms deeply. He even set the poem in two separate versions, the first of which uses cross-rhythms of three quavers against four as an expressive device to heighten the climax of the song, while the second contains that device, as a symbol of continuous agitation, throughout.

Other songs in this period suggest that the Schumanns were very much in Brahms's mind. Another Halm song, 'Bei dir sind meine Gedanken', Op. 95, no. 2, and also 'Auf dem Schiffe' (both 1884) to words by Reinhold, acknowledge that influence. The former is a clear reflection of Schumann's 'Berg und Burgen', written for Clara over forty years earlier. Both Brahms songs have that same key of A major and share the same imagery; in the first the thoughts of the loved one are like birds, while in the second the flying birds themselves symbolise feelings of release and escape. In both songs the accompaniment is pictorial, with a flutter of semiquavers varied in the second by the sustained buoyancy of upward arpeggios as the flight is borne aloft by the morning wind. Even the personal love-music of this phase seems distant and remote. Flight and song continually go together. In 'Es schauen die Blumen' (1884) Heine's lyrics fly to the loved one in soulful homage. In 'Nachtigall' by Reinhold (c. 1884) the melody combines with expressive staccato as the liquid notes fall like tears in an outpouring of regret for love lost long ago. Even the sensuality is less earthy, as in 'Schön war, das ich dir weihte', Op. 95, no. 7 (c. 1884), where the feeble and petulant words 'I might have hoped for a better reward for my love than this' elicit a similarly pallid response.

In 'Entführung', the expected song about waiting outside the loved one's house, the music is designed to be as forceful and heartless as the text (by Willibald Alexis). The frustrated lover, after six nights of bleak vigil, is now abducting the Lady Judith by main force, in hopes of a warmer response. There is a galloping vigour in the hard-driven piano part; and the far-ranging vocal line has (most unusually for Brahms) the wide interval of a rising tenth. As in 'Der Herr von Falkenstein', another encounter between woman and rider, there is good material here for an instrumental finale. But there is also a certain coldness and timidity at the heart of the song. The opening motto-theme with its attenuated Valkyrie-motif:

Ex. 21

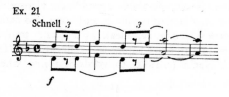

sounds curiously feeble, as if all that nocturnal exposure had taken its toll.

But this is a key song of 1884. The choice of poem shows the latent wish-fulfilment made manifest in music. The fading of thi sdream into real disillusion relates to other art-song themes; its continuance into further fantasy is reflected in folksong themes. In the former, the lady stays in the castle and the ageing lover remains alone with his memories, as in 'Mein Herz ist schwer' (1884). In the latter the young suitor is left outside in the cold, as in 'Vergebliches Ständchen' (c. 1881). If the girls find happiness in love or marriage ('Der Jäger', 'Mädchenlied', 'Dort in den Weiden', 'Vorschneller Schwur', all c. 1884) it is as it were off-stage, with other men. They too are most memorable when finally left lonely, as in 'Trennung'.

Take first the sad road of reality. In the Geibel 'Mein Herz ist schwer' the night winds moan through the trees as sad memories sigh through the mind, in a stormy alternation of 9/4 octaves. The rare time-signature and texture; the harmonic excursions (e.g. into A major from D flat, all with the tonic of G minor); the juxtaposition of dominant sevenths on G and E; all these are at least venturesome in their unsuccessful bid to recapture lost youth and vigour, as the poem says. In 'Steig auf, geliebter Schatten' (1884) the attempt and failure are both even more explicit. The funereal key of E flat minor; the weary descent of the themes in both voice and piano; the sombre foreshadowings of the *Serious Songs* – all these make the final plea to be made young again sound more like a dying fall.

In 'Mit vierzig Jahren' (1884) a poem of middle age looking back on life is translated into music of old age looking forward to death. The shift and focus of intensity are impressive. As the closing words speak of entering harbour, the harmony enters the tonic major on a full tide of deep rolling arpeggios, a heaven-haven of peace and fulfilment. But this is no facile acquiescence; the real struggle is revealed in the ominous octaves heard at the mention of going downhill which again prophesy the *Serious Songs*. This longed-for spiritual home or harbour of the imagination compensates for its absence from the real world; hence no doubt the choice of Halm's otherwise unmemorable verses 'Kein Haus, keine Heimat' (1884). This brief lament for house and homeland makes a laconic and comfortless recitative, bleak as a blank tombstone. This defiant negation turns to a supine self-abnegation in 'Der Tod, das ist die kühle Nacht' (c. 1884), to words by Heine, where the sense of contemplative detachment becomes other-worldly. The typical spread chords in the left hand, growing from the successively darker and deeper bass notes already used singly to evoke the cool night of death in the first line, beautifully evoke the idea of a dream from which there will be no awakening.

The other path, towards the world of folksong, traverses still more fertile terrain. In marked contrast to 'Entführung', the lover's unsuccessful plea for admission is treated with humour in 'Vergebliches Ständchen', no. 4 of Op. 84 (*c.* 1881). The buoyant opening melody is designed to impress the listener, whether the imagined girl or the actual audience, with a sense of lively immediacy. Hence the insistent rhythm, which is forced across the natural scansion of the text; hence too the sequential treatment. A pure lyric inspiration can also quite naturally take cerebral forms in Brahms. Here is how, consciously or not, a master-craftsman shapes his material:

Ex. 22

Each verse is treated as a variation on this theme. The music moans low in the minor, a man outside in the cold; and then laughs in the major, a woman inside in the warm. Finally the window is clapped firmly shut on a decisive sforzando chord. But so friendly a song cannot be an occasion for quarrel; the two will meet again next day. Similarly the girl in 'Der Jäger' (1884) confirms in the most affable of moods that proper access is not through the cottage door at night but through the church door by day. The musical humour is literally off-beat, an idea which recurs in 'Dort in den Weiden' (*c.* 1884) – a song worth comparing in detail with its folksong counterpart (no. 31 of the *49 Volkslieder*) to show how the art-song is constructed with more conscious artifice.

The same comparison illuminates other songs which exist in art and folk versions. 'Spannung', Op. 84, no. 5 (*c.* 1881), is a resetting of a supposed folksong already arranged by Brahms (as no. 4 of the *49 Volkslieder*). Its words are no doubt genuine. They treat tenderly of a love menaced by slander and scorn yet rising at last triumphant over all hazards – as in 'Von ewiger Liebe'. The original melody seems to be at least partly the work of Brahms's contemporary Anton von Zuccalmaglio. But something about it appealed to Brahms; perhaps the fact that each verse fortuitously ends, at the words 'my angel', with the B minor phrase which seems to have conveyed the idea 'Clara' to Brahms as to Schumann. The later setting includes such unfolklike devices as the use of augmented and diminished intervals in the voice and rhythmic variation in the piano, together with an optional added voice part in the concluding bars. Brahms clearly imagines this and other dialogues ('Vergebliches Ständchen' and the three Schmidt mother-and-daughter songs) as quasi-dramatic scenas; he published all five in one opus – 84 – 'for one or two voices and pianoforte'. In the masterly 'Trennung' (*c.* 1884) he achieves the feat of uniting the scene and character and expressive subtlety of the *Lied* with the unaffected simplicity of folksong. Again there are two versions. Both the poem and the melody of the original (No. 6 of the *49 Volkslieder*) seem to be entirely authentic, and Brahms's accompaniment finely sustains and sets off their artless appeal. The solo song offers further refinement. The slow quavers run unceasingly like the sad streams in the valley below ('da unten im Tale läuft's Wasser so trüb') which in turn are an image of ceaseless tears. The melodies too are diverted to flow downwards in voice and piano. The words are repeated for further emphasis. Thus in the first verse we hear a sweetly resigned phrase (Ex. 3 (*c*)) to the words 'i hab di so lieb' which themselves sound so innocent and vulnerable in their soft dialect form. A sad undercurrent of feeling is set surging throughout each successive verse. Whatever the words at each further repetition – 'I must go my ways' . . . 'I hope you fare better elsewhere' – we hear an underlying echo of 'I love you so much'. There are other subtle and tender touches, such as a suspicion of false relation at 'a bissele Falschheit ist auch wohl dabei'. Under a tranquil surface of simplicity there are profound and disturbed depths of feeling.

The last main song-writing period continues to be notable for maturity of technique. Even the occasional songs have a mellow gloss, like carefully tended silverware. A shining example is the highly wrought 'Komm bald', which was finished in a single day in May 1885. Klaus Groth had sent Brahms the poem as a birthday token of affection and esteem. But the next day the complete song had been written and posted to their mutual friend, the soprano Hermine Spies, who had also received a copy of the verses from their author. The verses were hardly more than an agreeably worded post-card – 'The garden's looking lovely just now, full of bloom; wish you were here'. The kind thought is illustrated in full rich chords and an appealing melody. Perhaps it is the idea of flowers and friendship, achievement and fulfilment, that so suffuses this music with an Indian summer of warmth and colour. Certainly Brahms was by this time fully aware of his mastery of the song form and its place at the heart of his work. He now writes songs about his songs ('Meine Lieder', Op. 106, no. 4) and music about his music ('Wie Melodien zieht es', Op. 105, no. 1), both 1886. The latter poem, again by Klaus Groth, offers a rather obscure conceit about the ground of language, that dark soil whence a deep thought could grow into either a word or a tone. In Brahms's language it becomes not only a song but the first movement of the A major Violin Sonata, Op. 100:

Ex. 23

That whole work is also full of 'Komm bald' and other late songs, in a musical repertory of retrospect and valediction. But there are fewer tragic love-songs. It seems that unrequited devotion is losing the power to hurt and gaining in power to ennoble. Even the bitter reproaches sound sweet. 'I doubt if you have a heart', says Fleming in 'An die Stolze' (1886); but the warm music has heart enough for two. 'Maienkätzchen', by Liliencron (1886), needs thorough study before being recognised as a song of separation; as in 'Trennung', love outweighs sorrow. The latter song is recalled in the parallel thirds of 'Klage' (1886), Brahms's last authentic folk-song setting to have an opus number (Op. 105, no. 3). Such a song in earlier years would have been in the minor throughout; this one begins and ends in a reconciled and forgiving major tonality. Similarly the avowedly cheerful songs have an added gaiety or nonchalance. 'Das Mädchen spricht' (1886) is frankly popular music. What inspires the swallow's tender morning song, wonders the girl in Gruppe's poem. Two pairs of rhythmic figures, to right and left of the keyboard, brush and skim like wings; but the chord and harmonies are full and round, robust rather than delicate. In this song a favourite symbolism finally comes home to roost; the lives and loves of birds and humans are warmly identified.

The student songs that began in Göttingen and continued in the *Akademische Fest-Overtüre* now graduate in the artistry of Kugler's 'Ständchen' (also 1886). Its counterpoint and other academic devices have a worldly and sophisticated lilt. 'Salamander' (1886) is rather less compelling. The legendary beast that feels at home in fire is thrown therein by a wicked girl; and is then seen to be really in his element. Words and music just fail to make a witty point, the former because of Lemcke's ineptitude, the latter because of Brahms's essential seriousness. But this erotic vein though middle-aged still has a perceptible and lively pulse. The gipsy music first hinted at in 'Magyarisch' of twenty years earlier bursts out in full-blooded élan in the Hungarian settings of supposed folk poems translated by Hugo Conrat, *Zigeunerlieder*, Op. 103, originally composed for vocal quartet (1887).

The typical phrase at 'Czardasmelodie beginnt' might have supplied title as well as theme-song for a successful operetta; and these sumptuous tunes did in fact make Brahms a small fortune. The mood and music of boots and spurs that shine and jingle must have struck responsive chords in many a middle-aged fantasy-life; and would still do so in suitably restrained yet invigorating performance. In Brahms's own mind the response was perhaps sadder. The strains of rebuff, ostracism, defeat, despair, are still heard, including the theme of being left out in the cold – literally, in Groth's 'Es hing der Reif', Op. 106, no. 3 (1886). There the mood of musing coldness takes on a marmoreal quality like a memorial in music. The dreaming arpeggios in the left hand, answering to the direction 'träumerisch'; the incantatory effect of repeated rhythmic patterns interrupted only by declamation which heightens that effect; the apparent allusion to the climax of 'Der Doppelgänger' as in 'Herbstgefühl', all this paints an impressively bleak picture of a winter landscape of the heart. In 'Verrat' (1886) the singer once more waits outside, this time to kill a rival, in what is surely the most powerful ballad of revenge in all *Lied* literature. Only at this late stage could Brahms treat Lemcke's theme with the necessary detachment. It may even be by a deliberate stroke of dramatic irony that this dark song of murderous jealousy and broken troth should begin with a hint of the prelude to 'Von ewiger Liebe'.

'Ein Wanderer' (1886) sounds somewhat like the expiation of those guilty thoughts. In Reinhold's poem the wayfarer's road of sorrow is signposted, by the usual ominous octaves, to his destination of death. The music moves in heavy-laden but purposeful strides to its desired end. In Liliencron's 'Auf dem Kirchhofe' (1886) the churchyard becomes less of a quiet resting-place than a sanatorium, whence the occupants depart healed – a sentiment which Brahms treats with scrupulous earnestness and fair success. His own desire for peace after strife, haven after storm, is again manifest. Even the gentle swing and sway of a tranquil life and love are left far behind in 'Auf dem See' (1886), another life-renouncing poem by Reinhold. Love-song and barcarolle glide along together in sinuous melodic lines and rocking arpeggios until finally the six-eight rhythm broadens to three-four, the spread semiquaver notes thicken to full quaver chords, thus slowing and steadying the movement as the 'floating Eden' heads for its last moorings.

If treated with undue warmth, all this music could easily curdle into a glutinous sentimentality. Given coolness and restraint it retains a fresh perfection of form and substance. Its Brahmsian yearning for release and relief in some translunar paradise of the imagination is far from any morbid death-wish. The composer at 53 was still eleven years away from immortality, and in no special hurry. The music tells us something of the peace and serenity within his own mind. This in turn allows him to contemplate all emotional life with a new sympathy.

In 'Immer leiser wird mein Schlummer' (1886) a woman near to death sings to her faithless lover, 'If you would see me once again, then come soon; soon'. Again the music absorbs and neutralises the sentimentality of the lyric, by Hermann Lingg. On the last page the fluid syncopations, the shifting tonalities of the six-four chords, spread in dream-like arpeggios, paint an unforgettable picture of drifting away from life as a cloud sifts into space. The absence of right-hand accent, the absence of chords in root position, the absence of clear progression, all converge to vanishing point.

In the more modest 'Mädchenlied' (1886) Heyse's deserted girl spinning in vain at her wedding finery sings, consciously or not, the five-note B minor theme associated with Clara, now in her thirtieth year of widowhood. The steady spinning in the accompaniment is a meditation on the skein of fate, with its separate strands of sweetness and sadness, major and minor.

1894-96: Last Songs

By 1886 all the threads had begun to draw together. The folk or popular themes and styles were embodied in the fabric of the art-song, and conversely. The Heyse 'Mädchenlied', the ballad 'Verrat', the love-lyrics 'Maienkätzchen' and 'An die Stolze', all offer to speak for the people, and with their own voice. But Brahms was no mere spokesman or interpreter. All his life he believed with a passionate humility, the more impressive for being so rarely mentioned, that he was really a plain man, at best a knowing craftsman. In his work the artist and the artisan form a union.

All these years he had been quietly compiling and perfecting his folksong arrangements. There is no evidence that these were completed in their published order. But the 1894 collection of *49 Deutsche Volkslieder mit Klavierbegleitung* shows a master hand gradually taking a whole national genre within an ever surer musical grasp in which strength turns to tenderness and delicacy of touch. The conspiratorial asides of the girl in 'Wie komm ich denn zur Tür herein?' offer a selection of keys and gestures as ways of opening the door. 'Lift the latch gently, so that mother will think it's the wind rattling':

Ex. 24

– the simplest and most insinuating of all Brahms's themes of nocturnal entry into houses and affections. In 'Ich weiss mir ein Maidlein' there are little tender musing interludes which take over from and seemingly contradict the words. 'Don't trust her, she's making a fool of you', says the voice; and so she may, and welcome, says the piano.

In the magnificent 'In stiller Nacht', not only the rhythmically complex accompaniment (expressively simplified and changed to a unison with the voice at the words 'Ein Stimm beginnt zu klagen', etc.) but also most of the melody seems to have been written by Brahms himself. This work deserves an honoured place among his original *Lieder*. Lament and loneliness in the night had been favourite themes from 'Die Mainacht' onwards: and a whole life-time of such thoughts and impulses went into this music, which is ennobled and dignified by the last-period idea that suffering is not merely personal but is shared.

In general the last three books of the *49 Volkslieder* contain all the oldest and best authenticated of melodies. According to Max Friedländer,[1] 'All mein Gedanken' (no. 30) dates from 1460, 'Es steht ein Lind' (no. 41) from 1550, 'Du mein einzig Licht' (no. 37) from 1648. The older Brahms grows, we feel, the deeper his sources; high growth needs firm roots.

This sense of natural fulfilment was deeply rooted in his own mind. In sending these volumes to Clara Schumann, and thence to his publisher, Brahms wrote 'I expect you noticed that the last of the songs [i.e. 'Verstohlen geht der Mond auf'] occurs in my Op. 1 ?' (the C major Piano Sonata, where it is the theme of the slow movement). 'And did anything else come to your mind? It was in fact designed to say something, it was intended to represent the snake that bites its own tail, and thus to express symbolically the idea that the tale is over, the circle completed.'

The choice of metaphor is revealing. So is the choice of work; so is the fact that its words and melody seemed just as genuine to Brahms at sixty as at twenty, whereas from a purely literary or sociological point of view both were clearly of dubious authenticity. Why did the obviously artificial verses mean so much to him? Two true hearts under the moon, a sweet sentimental sampler embroidered with silver clouds and roses and forget-me-nots, depicting home and country, house and garden; this was the illustrated family reading of the whole nineteenth century. But that is the world of Brahmsian song, created from unassuaged passion and dedicated devotion. His music finds and illuminates

[1] *Brahms' Lieder* (Berlin and Leipzig, 1922), pp. 184-9.

the reality behind the sentiment. His art embraces both lovers, man and woman, in life and death. Much frustration and loneliness went into that warm knowledge, much corrective bitterness into those sweet thoughts.

This then is the world and the mind that formed the *Vier ernste Gesänge (Four Serious Songs)*, Op. 121, in which they find their deepest and most durable expression. The *Ernste Gesänge* were written in 1896, the first original songs for ten years. What had breathed such new spirit into a composer who had already given up the ghost? Of course the themes of love and death were always dear to him, heart and soul. But here is something more; a sense of an unusually powerful concentration on language, and of a deep outgoing concern for all humanity. Brahms happened to live some thirty years longer than Schubert, some twenty years longer than Schumann or Wolf. His experience thus went far beyond theirs. Luther's Bible, we feel, spoke to him directly. It has a stark simplicity denied to rhythmically more complex forms. It rings even truer than folksong itself; it blends the direct speech of two peoples, German and Jewish. Its meaning and its sonorities are alike magnificent – and sometimes alien from the Authorised Version. Thus 'the evil work that is done under the sun' is not on the face of it an idea one much wishes to say Amen to. But in Luther's German 'Das Böse . . . das unter der Sonne geschieht' has a cadence of acceptance and submission. Life is thus; its will be done. For this cadence Brahms writes the perfect music, including an element of diffidence and dissonance which makes the final resolution seem even more serene. Again, 'O death, how acceptable is thy sentence' offers little of the soothing simplicity of 'O Tod, wie wohl tust du', where the long vowels turn naturally into long notes to make a fine melody and a fine end.

But even at this stage of verbal wisdom Brahms is still capable of constructing songs from spare parts: and this song-writing phase, like most of the others, contains some typical pasticcio. Of the *Four Serious Songs*, the last (fine though it is) is usually felt to be the least compelling. Unlike the first three, it lacks the sense of being the definitive expression of its text, St Paul's sermon on charity from the first Epistle to the Corinthians (13: 1-13). And we learn from Max Kalbeck[1] that it is in fact patched with material from earlier unfinished works, the words and putative

[1] *Johannes Brahms*, IV (Berlin, 1914), pp. 449-50.

dates of which leave little doubt of their origins in feelings of un-requited love for Elisabeth von Herzogenberg. Its opening phrase began as a setting of a poem called 'Trauerlied' by Rückert, about life's disappointments and frustrations. The calm close of the first section in E flat major borrows a melody from a setting of Keller's 'Nixe im Grundquell', where the imagery would have an especial appeal for Brahms – 'My heart is a calm lake, fed by the warm secret spring in which you bathe, my golden-haired water-nymph'. This blue and gold seascape with bathing nymphs must surely have come from the same gallery as the Heine 'Mondenschein' and others which depict the same scene. Finally the closing vocal cadence echoes many a song of blissful love, notably 'Wie bist du meine Königin', as if Brahms is taking 'the greatest of these is love' as his text for a decidedly unPauline epistle addressed to *amor* rather than *caritas*. The middle section's modulation to B major and the harplike adagio arpeggios are more spiritual, recalling 'Mit vierzig Jahren' and its final voyage to the desired haven.

Though some of the material thus originates in or derives from earlier songs, this one is no less a masterpiece for that. From what-ever mine of meaning the musical ores were first taken, they were always essentially right in substance and are now refined to the utmost purity of musical expression. The frustration and energy released from the Rückert poem gives added impetus to the open-ing ideas of having charity yet profiting nothing. The love-worship and mystery of Keller may not be an exact spiritual equivalent of St Paul; but in their way they too may offer true insight into the nature of charity. Brahms was unlikely to be mistaken in believing that his earlier music was apt to this later purpose. And his crafts-manship is impecacable. In ways too manifold for detailed illustra-tion, all the materials, old and new, are welded into a strong and a seamless unity. If one example can stand for many, then let it be these prodigious arches of melody which span the bridge passage leading back to the final *adagio* 'the greatest of these is charity'.

Ex. 25

A bass voice of full compass and resonance can say in itself, in these seven bars, that here are three great things, and that the last is the strongest yet the tenderest of all; and indeed that its strength lies in its tenderness. At the same time the sharply falling octaves in the left hand, the slowly rising phrases in the right, the far-reaching intervals in the voice, the long high note and falling tone on 'Liebe', are all motivically interrelated with the rest of the song, so that each successive or simultaneous idea supports and enhances the others in a paean of cumulative exaltation.

Even more resplendent are the three other *Serious Songs*. As we have seen their idiom had been anticipated here and there. So had their topics of death and resignation, *passim*. Yet they are in every sense original compositions; and they sound new notes of grandeur and nobility, evoking ideas of orchestration (for which sketches exist). But Brahms must have felt that these last words of wisdom and compassion are more at home in the intimate and domestic world of the *Lied* and the ideal of life in music shared with Clara Schumann. Age brought them even closer together in mutual comfort for their sorrows.

Elisabeth von Herzogenberg had died in 1892, Hermine Spies in the following year. Death was taking even the nightingales. In 1894 Brahms's old friend Billroth died, in 1895 Clara's friend Livia Bendemann. Soon Clara's daughter Marie was ill. Her son-in-law had a stroke. Expressions of solicitude and condolence fall autumnally thick in these last years, helping to soften the blows. Yet these two old friends, in an age notable for Christian piety, maintained a stoic silence about the consolations of religion. No word survives about life after death; there is no breath of any such belief. Between the lines of the letters lies the text 'all go unto one place; all are of the dust, and all turn to dust again'.

In March 1896, Clara had a slight stroke. In April she rallied; Brahms wrote to Marie, 'Your mother gave us all a great fright'. In May she was able to scrawl a few touchingly vague and illegible words of greeting for his birthday, which she had never once left uncelebrated since their first meeting more than forty years earlier. In the same month came a fatal relapse. In the same month too the *Four Serious Songs* were completed. Perhaps they were all begun before Clara's first illness in March. But even so, sentiment does not preclude presentiment; quite the contrary. Brahms surely knew that his Clara's days were numbered.

Soon he would follow her to the grave, leaving these songs to hymn those deaths, and that love, and the human condition. At first hearing the greatest of these is death. The prelude of 'Denn es gehet dem Menschen wie dem Vieh' takes us back, at a drum-stroke, into the *German Requiem*. The repeated dominant in the piano part tolls like a passing bell, twenty-six times in the first nine bars, with no variant save for a sad semitonal sigh at 'beast' and 'dies'. The music is made to tread and breathe like great black oxen. At 'vanity' the dust rises in a quick swirl and flurry of diminished seventh harmonies and detached arpeggios, and is then laid again, while the bell of quittance in the left hand still intones without respite. The text debates whether the spirit of man goeth upward. But the music, all doubt, has no doubt. The strong gestures of denial in both hands insist that man dieth even as the beast; even so. And the incessant labouring tread of the march returns to say that there is nothing better than for a man to re-joice in his own works, for that is his portion.

The song could have ended there. But Brahms was impelled to express the ominous words that follow – 'for who shall bring him to see what shall be after him?' Perhaps he felt as one about to die, leaving no widow or child; 'kein Weib und kein Kind' as the poem he chose for Op. 94, no. 5, tells us, in the same key of D minor. Then what shall be after him, the music asks despairingly; what of his works will survive? Nothing, as like as not, is the comfortless answer. The dust flies about as before, this time in all directions, in contrary motion; and at last settles on to a featureless desert of repeated bass notes and the final bleak questioning of an empty fifth, expecting the answer 'no'. There is no trace here of the complacency of 'Abendregen'; the future holds no rainbows now. A song which began by joining a funeral procession ends by facing total annihilation. But it does so in courage and defiance, as the work of a man who can truthfully say *in extremis* that he has given the best he has to give, and who here presents it, come what may, with outstretched hands in two final crashing chords.

In 'Ich wandte mich' the piano prelude moves down in hollow octaves into darkness, meaning (in the Brahmsian language of music) Death. Later this same motif is used to celebrate first the dead and then, in the diminished seventh harmonies which in the previous song savoured so bitterly of dust and ash, the unborn state of not-being. This, the best of all for man, is tellingly signified by a long silence. The contrasting theme is also simplicity itself, a warm rounded phrase meaning weeping and lamentation which in turn is inflected in different rhythms and registers to make a whole new vocabulary of sorrow and sympathy. And these two very different elements are compounded in a reconciling and accepting major tonality at the last phrase which finally praises the world despite its manifold evils.

In the last song of death, 'O Tod wie bitter bist du', lies the consummation of all Brahms's song-music. That mighty contra-puntal brain is still at work focusing and illuminating its images. The bitterness of death to some is contrasted with its comfort to others; and we are shown how these two opposed faces wear the same expression.

Ex. 26

These intervallic subtleties are juxtaposed with the simplest and sweetest of melodies, the most richly satisfying of motivic illustrations and contrasts. Compare, for just one example, the bluntly assertive piano rhythms, both hands greedily full, of 'him who still hath strength to receive meat' with the helplessly curved and frail vocal lines of 'him that is in extreme old age and hath lost strength'. Again all these disparate ideas are resolved in the closing section, where the voice's last four notes decline to a peaceful end and a long rest.

On these notes, with these sentiments, ends Brahms's life in song; indeed his own life, and that of the nineteenth-century *Lied*.